How To...

BY JEFF ADAMS

PLAY COUNTRY LEAD GUITAR

To access audio visit:
www.halleonard.com/mylibrary

Enter Code
8117-3173-9272-7949

ISBN 978-1-4803-9801-6

HAL•LEONARD® CORPORATION

7777 W. BLUEMOUND RD. P.O. BOX 13819 MILWAUKEE, WI 53213

Visit Hal Leonard Online at
www.halleonard.com

CONTENTS

INTRODUCTION

The country solo has grown from simplistic bass-string licks to a fast-paced onslaught of chromatic melodicism and technical variety. The sustaining sounds of pedal steel licks and ringing open strings mixed with the staccato clucks of chicken pickin' and punchy double stops that flow from the expressive fingers of today's session players and stars make country solos some of the most exciting guitar statements on the radio. The intoxicating appeal of their licks has been coveted by all six-stringers, but the knowledge of how to create the licks themselves has been reserved for the finely tuned ears of seasoned pros, leaving the intermediate players to wallow in pentatonic squalor.

Enter *How to Play Country Lead Guitar*. This volume is a comprehensive stylistic breakdown of country guitar techniques of the past 50 years. Drawing inspiration from the timelessly innovative licks of Merle Travis, Chet Atkins, Albert Lee, Vince Gill, Brent Mason, and Brad Paisley, the near 90 musical examples within these pages will hone your left and right hands with technical string-bending and rolling licks while sharpening your knowledge by exposing the thought process behind creating your own licks and why and when to play them. Whether you're an intermediate-level player wanting to add chicken pickin' flavors to your jazz lines or a rocker interested in dressing up your licks with chromatic sophistication and hybrid picking techniques, turn off the distortion, switch to your brightest pickup, and bring on the twang!

ABOUT THE AUDIO

Music examples accompany the lessons so you can hear what the material being taught sounds like. To access all of the audio examples that accompany this book, simply go to **www.halleonard.com/ mylibrary** and enter the code found on page 1. The examples that include audio are marked with icons and track numbers throughout the book.

ACKNOWLEDGMENTS

The pages of this book could not have been filled without the generous experiential wisdom of Chad Johnson and the open-ended support of the Hal Leonard staff. With your help, my ideas are made clear, credible, and entertaining to the world! Thank you.

CHAPTER 1: TONE

The ideal country tone is expressive yet consistent and fat yet bright with a capacity for note clarity. The recipe for this delicate balance is a time-tested formula of a Telecaster and a tube amp with compression and delay pedals in between. Sifting through the myriad of options in the typical instrument retailer can become a tedious experience, with a motivated salesman offering their advice, so the following pages are presented to simplify your choices. Each cited piece of gear has become a crucial mainstay in country players' pedal boards, guitar cases, and credited recordings.

GUITAR

The most iconic guitar on the market for country music is the Fender Telecaster. The image of James Burton's pink paisley while playing with Elvis and the twin guitars of Buck Owens and Don Rich solidified the instrument's popularity in the '60s, establishing it as the must-have axe for influential country pickers of the '90s, like Brent Mason, Brad Paisley, Keith Urban, Steve Wariner, and Vince Gill.

Be it a vintage Fender or a cost-conscious knock-off, this bare-bones guitar is an excellent starting point in any player's arsenal. The options that come stock with each instrument remain the same: a bright bridge pickup, a smooth-but-nasally neck pickup, and a fixed bridge. Each one of these attributes is perfect for all the country techniques presented in this book; the brightness of the bridge pickup perfectly emulates a pedal steel, and the fixed bridge makes the various bending techniques easier to execute. The recessed headstock also allows for behind-the-nut bends that increase the "twang" factor considerably. While those basic features remain the same from Tele to Tele, the variety of designs and enhancements—vintage saddles, multiple pickups, additional switches, its weight/wood type, etc.—should factor into your final assessment of the instrument.

What's ultimately important is connecting with the instrument you play. You're going to be spending many practice hours with it, so it must be a comfortable extension of your body. This includes the feel of the neck, how it sits in your lap, etc. The truly personal nature of playing guitar, or any instrument for that matter, makes the amalgam of wood, steel, and electronics that you have in your hands an often-overlooked choice of paramount importance to your (hopefully) long-lived relationship with music and the guitar.

AMP

The common amp choice of many country players has become a Fender-style tube amp, but they're not the only relevant choice. While the crisp and clean Fender Deluxe and Twin combo amps have been the favorites of Brent Mason and James Burton, Brad Paisley's Vox AC-30s and Keith Urban's Matchless combos give them the right amount of grit to fit their definitively unique styles. While their choices are varied, take comfort in the fact that they constantly change what amps they use based on their current musical interests; their choices are based on the sounds they hear in their head, and ideally, so should yours.

How to set your amp is a matter of personal taste and practicality. The treble, mid, and bass settings function in ways that balance each other out: the amount of bass you need is inversely proportionate to the treble, while the mids blend those frequencies together. A good setting to start out with is each parameter at 12 o'clock at a moderate volume. From there, strum and use your ears. If it's too bright, lower the treble. Too boomy? Lower the bass. When you're happy with each extreme, round out the mids to bridge the gap for an even response throughout the range of the guitar.

The perfect amp for you is what complements the instrument you have. Playing through the gear you are going to buy is imperative, as each amp reacts differently. Also, it's a good idea to bring your guitar to the store when you're testing out any piece of gear to hear and feel how it reacts. Try to emulate a specific recording of your favorite song, and you'll do fine. While there's no one perfect amp for all of country's varied sounds, I'd suggest finding a loud and clean amp, expanding your sound with pedals as necessary.

PEDALS

Now that you have a warm, fat sound as a base, it's time to add the icing. Pedals should add a deeper dimension to your tone. While you don't need these pedals to begin practicing (or even to be an authentic country picker), the qualities these little boxes add to your tone is all too intoxicating to ignore. Because of their allure, it's important to not go overboard, as too much of a particular effect can sound a bit juvenile. To avoid letting it become a crutch for your playing or lowering your amp's overall sound, we'll dissect the parameters of each pedal and outline how they're commonly used in a country context.

COMPRESSOR

One of the more well-known pedals to inhabit the pedal board of the modern country picker is the compressor. Because of the variety of picking articulations and need for clean sustain, country players use the compressor to even out their signal, thereby leveling out the peaks and boosting the softer notes for a pleasing and punchy sustain.

The most simplistic option is the two-knob pedal with *output* and *sensitivity* parameters. The sensitivity, now commonly referred to as "sustain," sets how long a note will last after it's picked.

MXR Dyna Comp with "output" and "sensitivity" controls.

Boss CS-3

The output, or "level," controls the volume of the signal once the pedal is active. Adjust this knob so that your volume doesn't drop when you turn the pedal on, as the amount of sensitivity has a tendency to lower the guitar's overall volume.

Evolving from the two-knob compressor, four-knob compressors enhance the sonic capabilities with attack and tone controls to add brightness and character despite the squeezing. To compensate for the sensitivity and attack, using the tone control to brighten the sound is a useful way to crisp things up. The attack regulates when the compression actually starts, serving as an "articulation-enhancer" of sorts—the lower the attack, the more even the response—because the compression is starting more quickly. With the attack at around 2 o'clock, you'll hear the pleasing twang, or the note's initial volume spike, because it's taking longer for the compression to start. It's only a matter of milliseconds, but that slight amount of time is particularly crucial for country's characteristic tone.

With all this complex processing happening, compression should be the first pedal in your signal chain. The next would be your distortions/overdrives, and then your time-based effects like chorus and...

DELAY

One of the most versatile effects behind the rhythm and lead guitar parts of most all popular music today is the delay pedal. With a tonal palette ranging from adding reverb-like sustain to creating an exacting illusion of doubled attacks, delay is an excellent first purchase to start off any pedal board because of its distinct impact on the sound in all styles.

Available in a wide variety of models with digital, analog, and vintage modeling capabilities, the parameters for delay come standardized as essentially output, feedback, and delay time controls. *Output* determines how loud the delayed sound is compared to your dry guitar signal; *feedback* controls the number of times the delayed signal repeats; and *delay time*, calculated in milliseconds, extends or shortens the time between the initial attack and the delayed signal(s). Because the process of getting each one of these controls to work in concert with one another is tediously time-consuming in the studio, the *tap tempo* feature (found in the more high-priced models) is worth the extra money in spared headaches.

Settings

What is colloquially referred to as "slapback" delay is an instant reflection of the signal when you set the delay time anywhere from approximately 50 to 150 milliseconds. The feedback is usually set to repeat from one to three times, and the output is at least half the guitar's dry input signal. Similar to reverb with a more precise decay, slapback works great when you play staccato, single-note passages. Because of delay's precision, the line retains its compressed sparkle while adding a gentle halo of atmospheric sustain.

TRACK 1

*Delay set to 50-150 milliseconds w/ 1-3 repeats.

Slapback delay with chicken pickin' lines like this adds more weight to the double stops and pronounces the muted triplets with extra punch.

TRACK 2

*Delay set to 50-150 milliseconds w/ 1-3 repeats.

Another interesting employment of delay is to have it set to sound like separate attacks, as heard in Albert Lee's classic solo from "Country Boy." With the output of the effect to match your guitar's signal and the feedback set for one repeat only, the setting for delay time is more complicated. There's a little math involved to get this effect in perfect tempo with the song at hand, but what we're going for is a straight series of 16th notes while picking only eighth notes (or a series of eighth notes while picking only quarter notes if you're playing a fast cut time). Here's what we do: Divide 60 by the song's tempo (converting the tempo to beats per second) and multiply that difference by 1.5 (making the effect repeat 1.5 beats later), effectively doubling the steady quarter-note rhythms you play to sound like eighth notes. Our next example is at 300 bpm (half note = 150), and here's how the calculation would look:

$60/300 = 0.2$

$0.2 \times 1.5 = 0.3$

"0.3" is now in seconds; to convert it to milliseconds, multiply that by 1000 to get a usable delay setting of 300 milliseconds.

Now that you've remembered why you hated high school math, let's have some fun with this by using the delay to help us play otherwise impossible lines at inhuman speeds. This delay setting is particularly useful when playing double stops, transforming what would normally be carpal tunnel-inducing position shifts into a perplexing but simple-to-execute sonic illusion.

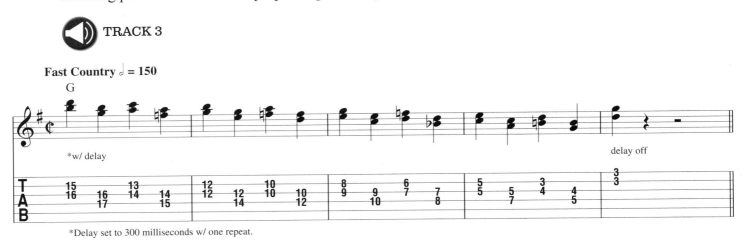

TRACK 3

Fast Country ♩ = 150

*w/ delay

delay off

*Delay set to 300 milliseconds w/ one repeat.

Right-Hand Options: Pick vs. Thumbpick

Due to the inspirational impact Merle Travis, Chet Atkins, Jerry Reed, Steve Wariner, and Brent Mason have had on the development of country music's soloing vocabulary, the use of the right hand has grown markedly complex, and the search for the right plectrum has become a crossroads for migrating rock and metal guitarists. Whether to retain their alternate picking chops by integrating the fingers into their technique or trade in their Jazz IIIs for a thumbpick and grow their nails for evenness of tone is another crucial choice for practicing consistency.

Each option presents hindrances that can be alleviated by devoted patience during practice, but the path of picking least resistance may not be the answer for the *sound* you're looking for. While a straight pick has less of a learning curve for adding your fingers into the mix, the thumbpick provides opportunities for wider stretches and impressive solo fingerstyle pieces. The thumbpick's fixed position on your hand is also a concern if your alternate picking speed is a result of "circle picking." Because the straight pick is controlled by at least two fingers, two digits are available for hybrid picking patterns, but anything more than plucking three notes at a time requires the pinky—the least-trainable finger.

Many other factors weigh into your ultimate pick of choice, but they're relatively cheap, so spend $4 or $5 and experiment with as many thicknesses and types of picks as possible in hopes of the most enjoyable playing experience.

Acrylic Nails

Many avenues have been explored in the unending search for tone—some practical, others not—from spending thousands of dollars maintaining vintage amps to even relic'ing a modern instrument for the road-worn look where it spends its days in a display case. One road less-traveled is that of getting regular manicures. That's right; the most relaxing indulgence for women has become a regular tone maintenance appointment for some of the best pickers in Nashville. Brent Mason and Johnny Hiland's frequent visits to the beauty parlor keep their tone consistent from their pick to their fake fingernails. While you can't argue with their results, the average bimonthly price of $35 might be a turn-off for the starving musician, so here are a few cost-effective solutions to try.

At a modest cost of around $7 per bottle, *nail hardener* provides home maintenance and convenience while having the benefit of using your own fingernails. Just let them grow to about 1/16-inch past the fingertip, shape to something similar as the guitar pick, and let the hardener do the rest. The result is even tone at a quarter of the price.

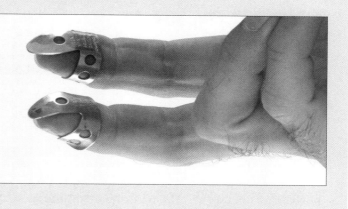

Another useful solution, tried and tested by the great James Burton, is fingerpicks. Primarily used by banjo and pedal steel players, fingerpicks maintain uniform tone with the plectrum without the tedious upkeep of fake fingernails. An added benefit is the less likely risk of mid-solo breaks when compared to the frailty and susceptibility of hardened nails to hot stage lights, humid outdoor temperatures, and sweaty palms.

CHAPTER 2: RIGHT-HAND TECHNIQUES

The musical ideas found in country guitar solos, fills, and hooks have a rich base in emulating other instruments. Pedal steel licks, banjo rolls, and chicken pickin' are musical onomatopoeias inspired by guitarists in search of a particular sound to give their solos more depth. The intrigue of the lines is based on the harmony and timbre of the notes, and those subtle articulation nuances are the essence of country guitar technique.

The right-hand techniques specifically capitalize on the expressive qualities of using the fingers in conjunction with the pick. The ability to simultaneously sound two or three notes with the fingers rather than a strum allows for a broader dynamic range of pick attack and a more personal touch to your lines.

HYBRID PICKING

Popularized by the exciting solo guitar music of Merle Travis, Chet Atkins, and Jerry Reed, fingerstyle music with walking bass lines and melodies all in one beautiful arrangement inspired the likes of Brent Mason and others to incorporate that nuance into the hooks and leads of late '80s and '90s country. Because of each one's use of the thumbpick in their finger-twisting licks, plectrum devotees were forced to unlock the right-hand potential of their otherwise dormant digits, leading to what's now referred to as *hybrid picking*.

The use of fingers in conjunction with the pick adds dimension to your playing when you competently perform fingerstyle riffs without changing your picking technique. The ability to fluidly add your fingers into your picking patterns is the ultimate test for the mastery of this technique. This section is essentially an abbreviated crash course in fingerstyle guitar adapted for the pick, so any fingerpicking books in your library can augment the techniques you develop here.

To start, it's recommended to slowly integrate your fingers into constant bass riffs. This bass line follows a root–3rd–5th–3rd pattern for the C chord (fifth-string root) and a root–5th–3rd–5th pattern for the G chord (sixth-string root). Focus on palm muting each note and making the string crossings automatic before moving on to the next step.

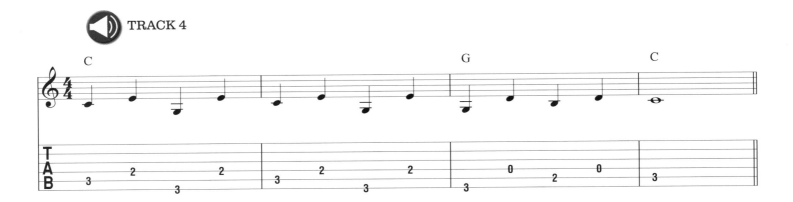

TRACK 4

Once your pick is a solid rock of rhythm, try adding your fingers to the riff. The sound of the riff is slowly becoming a full part, so it's tempting to speed the pattern up too early. But don't underestimate this stage: even though you're only adding two extra notes, the fingers don't know how to act yet, so starting slow and building up, yet again, is the rule of the day.

TRACK 5

In the previous example, the fingers pluck the B string notes on beat 2 and the "and" of 3 for a natural, folk-sounding pattern. But, our next example flips the fingerpicking to beats 1 and 3. This subtle yet crucial variation is like rubbing your head and patting your stomach once you've become comfortable with the first pattern.

TRACK 6

Another challenging obstacle for hybrid pickers, because there are primarily two strong digits for picking, is a three-note arpeggio in alternating bass patterns. To compensate for this, there are situations where the pick needs to play two notes at the same time, serving as the bass and melody notes. Play the following with just your pick, but angle your hand just enough to allow the G string to ring while muting the D string at the same time.

TRACK 7

*P.M. on strings 6-4 throughout.

Merle Travis actually pioneered this technique out of necessity. Because he only used his index finger for picking patterns, the double-duty of the thumbpick allowed for more exciting lines. In measure 1, beat 4 and measure 2, beat 2 of the next example, the pick plays both notes. Because of the palm muting on strings 6–4, the G string is still heard as the loudest-sounding note, keeping the melody intact.

TRACK 8

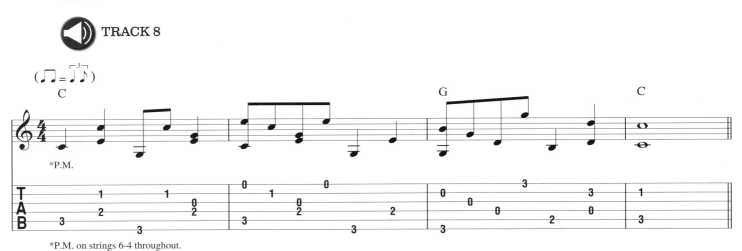

*P.M. on strings 6-4 throughout.

As you're building speed, you may find your fingers tripping over each other. If they disrupt the natural movement of the pick, your fingers need a little more fine-tuning. Carefully observe your right hand as you play to make sure your fingers move straight up and bend at the knuckle. This becomes tricky to train within the context of alternating bass and fingerpicked melodies, so take it slowly with this ragtime-inspired ditty. Carefully plot your left-hand fingering in measure 6 to keep the melody pronounced and the bass line muted. (Hint: you don't need to hold the F barre down after beat 2.)

TRACK 9

*P.M. on strings 6-4 throughout.

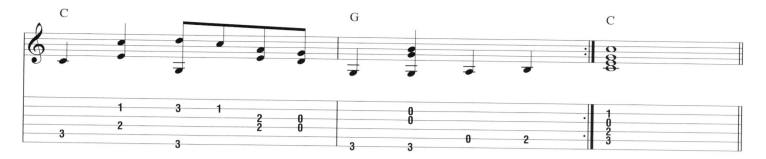

For something a little more modern, this motion becomes important for the speed and double stops of this 8-bar country blues shuffle in D.

TRACK 10

Moderately slow ♩ = 89

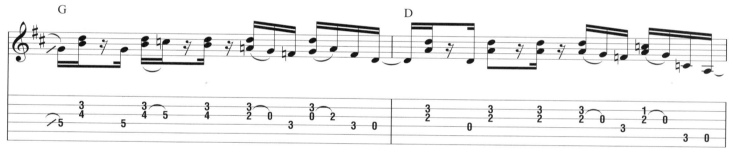

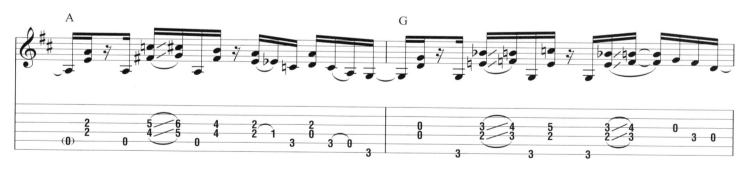

Using your fingers independently of the pick is not the singular advantage that hybrid picking affords. It also has the benefit of compensating for the defects in your picking technique. Most guitarists' alternate-picking technique is in an ever-constant state of improvement, so as your growth to become a technical monster is in progress, adding the fingers to your single-note lines is a useful temporary solution.

The scenarios where picking pitfalls are most prevalent are the cross-string phenomena known as *outside picking* and *inside picking*. *Outside picking* arises when a downstroke is followed by an upstroke on a higher string.

Play through this triplet-based, E Mixolydian lick and note beats 2 and 4 of measure 1, which are particularly challenging because of outside picking.

TRACK 11

These situations would typically be solved by *economy picking* (either an upstroke or downstroke followed by the same on neighboring strings), but the use of a finger or two removes the awkwardness of feeling stuck when the line goes back up to the first string while adding a bit of country twang to the line.

TRACK 12

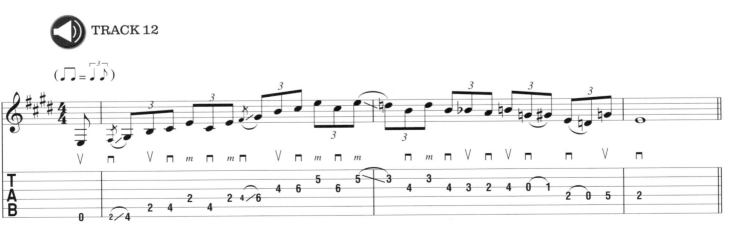

Inside picking is another lock of the pick's free movement resulting from a downstroke followed by an upstroke on a lower string.

Here's another low-string triplet lick in the key of E that demonstrates inside picking on beat 3, measure 1 and beat 1, measure 2. Once you play through the alternate picking, be creative and inject hybrid picking where you think it would be best applied. Adding hammer-ons and pull-offs in places is another solution to your speed woes.

🔊 TRACK 13

As you may have noticed, both of the inside/outside picking scenarios are present in each of these examples. Building your chops up for any musical situation should remain your ultimate goal, and the application of these techniques should primarily add to the value of your expression—not permanently compensate for your technical deficiencies.

Now that the value of hybrid picking has been thoroughly described and its technical problems analyzed, let's move on to the ideas that produce the sounds of country music.

BANJO ROLLS

Banjo rolls emulate the sound of the banjo by letting open strings and fretted notes ring together to create a cascading sound. Before we delve too deeply into the characteristics that make banjo rolls sound like their namesake, let's get into the technical challenges.

We'll start with the *forward roll*. The forward roll is a *p-m-a* (pick–middle–ring) pattern that moves from the sixth string to the first. Our first example starts the forward roll on each chord tone of an open G chord in succession. As you work through this and other examples, make sure that your right-hand fingers move as little as possible when shifting from one string to the next. It's also imperative that you let each note ring as long as possible (i.e., fingers don't move up too far, pick doesn't change its position, fret-hand stays in place, etc.).

Playing through the practice routine in the above example may seem monotonous, so to keep things somewhat fresh, try switching between chords for an extra challenge. Chords with sixth-string roots have four rolls per chord, and fifth-string roots have three.

The *backwards roll* requires the most practice time, because starting with your ring finger is the furthest digit from your pick, and the muscle memory is far less developed. Its neglected development is similar to the upstroke of alternate picking—everyone's upstroke is weaker than their downstroke. To give the technique equal attention, let's try it on a G chord.

As you play through the next example, keep in mind the pitfalls akin to forward rolls: crossing strings, fingers moving too far up or in, etc. Also, these examples may not sound like banjo rolls just yet, but we're attempting to isolate the rolling aspect of the technique, so concentrate on your right hand as you play.

TRACK 16

Combining the forward and backwards rolls is another crucially fundamental facet of muscle memory to develop.

TRACK 17

The challenge here is when the pattern changes to a backwards roll. On the forward roll, each finger plays the next string; when the backwards rolls begin to take over, the pick and ring finger play the same note. Be careful to not allow your pick or fingers to trip over each other at this point. Slow and perfect repetition at gradually increasing tempos with a metronome is the M.O., as is the case with any practice routine.

Here's a droning banjo exercise moving through all inversions of a G7 chord to get your practical banjo technique underway.

TRACK 18

Now that the mechanics of the technique are under your fingers, let's apply them to a few country-style banjo rolls.

One of their most common uses is to imply *extended harmonies* (9th, 11th, 13ths, etc.) by horizontally climbing the neck. Here's a triplet-based lick ascending an E9 arpeggio with banjo rolls that ends with a bluesy Mixolydian descent. Beats 1 and 2 take advantage of open strings, each serving unique harmonic functions. As we're in the key of E, the open D string serves as the ♭7th, while the open G string is utilized as a chromatic passing tone to the G♯ of beat 3.

TRACK 19

Here are two more that incorporate intermediary arpeggios on beats 2 and 4 between the more obvious chord spellings on beats 1 and 3.

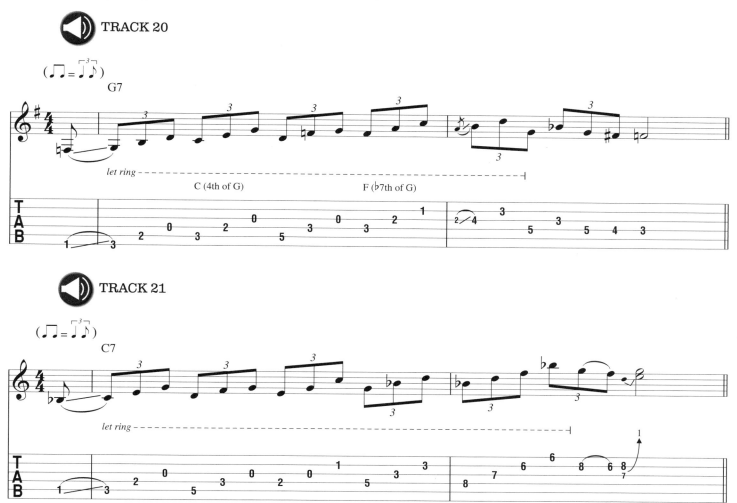

Here's a classic banjo roll, inspired by "Foggy Mountain Breakdown," that has now become a requisite technical development exercise for banjo players with guitars in their hands. The lick opens with a chromatic walk-up from the 3rd to the 5th in triple-stop form, necessitating wide stretches in prep for the rolling exercise that ensues. Tricky hammer-ons start measure 2, followed by a backwards banjo roll through strings 3–1 with unison G notes on the B and G strings. Letting the rolls ring into each other is crucial for the effect, so get comfortable with the four-fret stretch and perform the hammer-ons with your third and fourth fingers. Measure 4 reverses the chromatic 5th–3rd descent with strategically placed G and C pedal tones before addressing the 3rd to close the lick. Putting measures 2 and 4 on infinite loops with a metronome as your time-keeper is a surefire way to tighten your right- and left-hand technique.

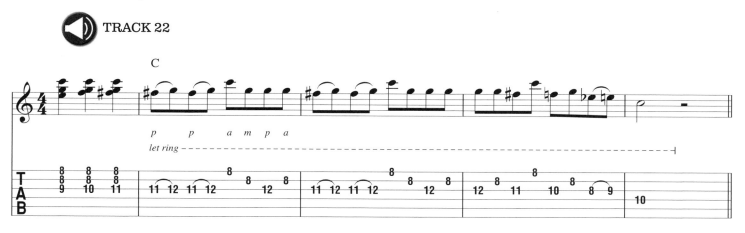

CHICKEN PICKIN'

The most recognizable sound that country guitar has contributed to the general lexicon of soloing techniques is *chicken pickin'*. A blend of muted and sustained articulations, this quick mix of the extremes of technical articulation has its basis in emulating a rooster with the guitar.

Now that your hybrid picking chops have been augmented with banjo rolls to subtly get your ring finger in shape, you're ready to tackle the "bak, bak, bak-awk" of chicken pickin'. Here's a typical application of this technique with a descending, rapid-fire triplet lick based in the E Mixolydian mode.

TRACK 23

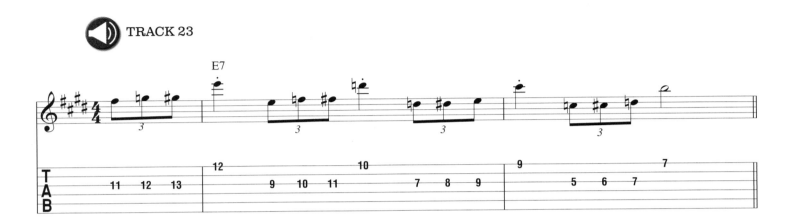

What's happening here is that we're sliding a 6th shape up to a target note (3rd) while barely fretting the notes to produce quick, muted notes on the upbeats. On the downbeats, the E string is plucked with the ring or middle finger.

On the technique side of things, there are two options for optimum performance. If you opt for using fingers in your single-note lines, a *p–m–p–a* picking approach is best. If you're an alternate-picking master, your hard-earned technical facility can handle the triplets on the G string, but use your middle or ring finger on the E string to give it that extra pop.

It's also common and effectively practiced to pluck a single note while muting it in between downbeats. It's not necessary to go between extremes of register for effectiveness. The real character of the technique is the mix of muted and sustained notes.

Here, we have chromatically descending 3rd shapes on the G and B strings built from the A Mixolydian mode. Use your pick for the muted notes on the G string and your finger for the notes of the B string to keep the pickin' poppin'. By using both pick and fingers for this descent, we're also avoiding an outside picking scenario which would more than likely trick the pick.

TRACK 24

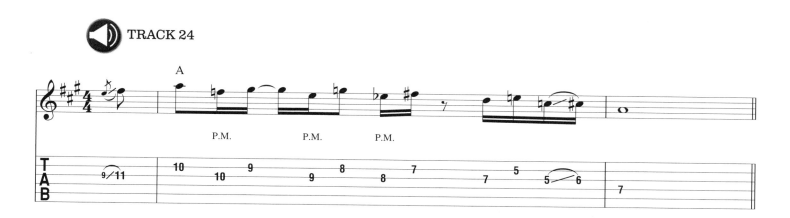

Adding another hair to the technical sides of things, this next example alters the pick and finger dynamic of chicken pickin' by adding double stops. This first-position lick in E minor pentatonic slides into the 5th/♭7th of E (B/D) on the G and B strings and rocks back and forth by plucking both strings with the second and third fingers and picking the muted G string. Making sure the pick and fingers don't trip over each other should be a concern, so it's helpful to downstroke from the wrist and pluck upwards from the knuckles.

TRACK 25

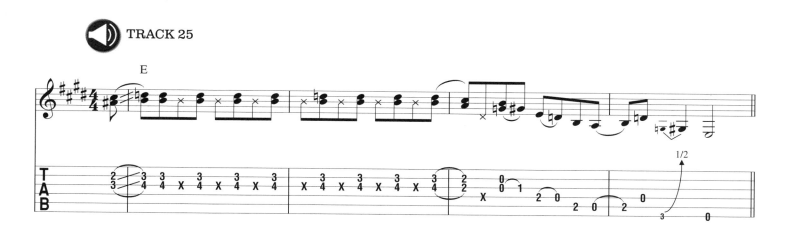

TWANG

From the opening notes of Johnny Cash's "Folsom Prison Blues" to the intro riff from "Chattahoochee" by Alan Jackson, twang's role in the creation of classic country hooks is ever-memorable and unmistakable.

The wound strings and low-register notes allow for the longer string to slap against the fretboard, creating a pleasing pop that, when coupled with compression, is the quintessence of country. One way to accentuate this effect is by picking closer to the bridge. Widening the distance between the fretted note and where you pick effectively lengthens the string and allows it to vibrate for longer. Depending on how hard you pick or pop the strings, the greater the potential for them to slap against the frets.

Pick as close to the bridge as you can on this twangy, bass-string romp, which is reminiscent of Pete Anderson's solo from "Guitars, Cadillacs" by Dwight Yoakam.

TRACK 26

Country Shuffle ♩ = 172

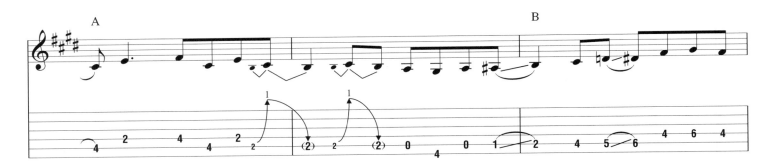

While the wound strings are great for low-note twang, the higher strings have an advantage, too. Consider the following lick. The notes are the exact same but are plotted in different parts of the neck. Example A, set at the ninth position, has a rounder timbre, which is great for a longer descent of double stops due to its position. Example B starts at the fourth position for a twangier sound, due to the length of the string.

TRACK 27

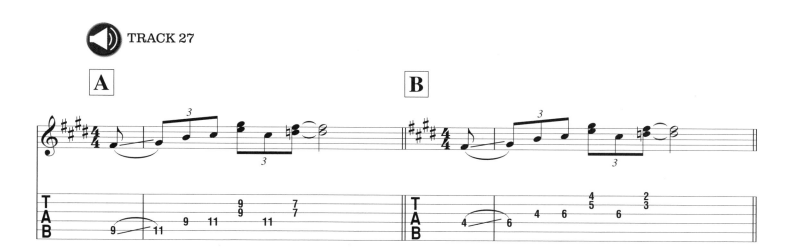

Baritone Guitar

Taking the "longer the string, the more twang" principle to the extreme, the *baritone guitar* mixes the comparable range of the bass with the twangy brightness of the guitar. With a *scale length* (distance from the saddle to the nut) about two inches longer than a standard guitar, baritone guitars are tuned a 4th lower—(low to high) B–E–A–D–F♯–B—for bright, low-end twang.

Heard in the intro from Glen Campbell's "Galveston" and all over "Suds in the Bucket" by Sara Evans, the baritone guitar's tight, bright, and low-end timbre is a unique texture for adding fatness to doubled lines and taking leads that hit impossible lows.

CHAPTER 3: LEFT-HAND TECHNIQUES

The role of the left hand is primarily charged with maintaining the balance between staccato and sustain—fought so hard by the practice of right-hand techniques. Manifesting as pedal steel bends and open-string licks, the necessary sensitivity to be developed for these techniques is finger-bending independence and overall fret-hand control. In concert with this intense physical conditioning, this chapter heavily deals with fretboard awareness along with the theoretical construction and application of those techniques.

PEDAL STEEL LICKS

The mechanics of the pedal steel guitar allow for chords to move from a minor harmony to a major sound while sustaining that same chord. It is essentially a slide guitar set on a table with pedals or knee-levers that stretch some of its ten strings by varying degrees. When chords are sustained, the activated pedals and levers create close harmonies that are often difficult to emulate on the guitar, but it's possible to emulate some of them.

To get your hands in shape for this technique, let's get acquainted with unison bends. *Unison bends* consist of fretted and bent notes that match in pitch. They're useful because the lower note of the bend is a whole step, so you're training the physical memory of your hands and the musical recognition of your ears at the same time. Here's a walk-up exercise to get your left hand in shape.

TRACK 28

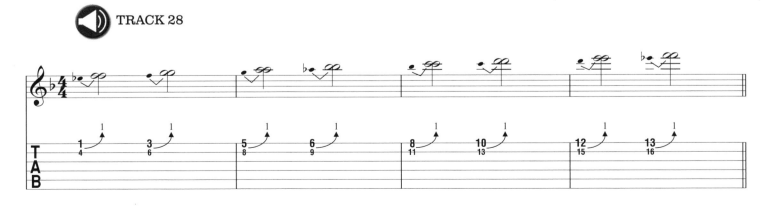

With your physical dexterity in check, a good way to train your ears for pedal steel licks is to write a line and then add the bends to it. This way, you'll get the sound of the lick in your head as a sort of aural preparation for adding the bends. To keep it somewhat simple at first, here's an F major scale in 3rds that moves up the neck.

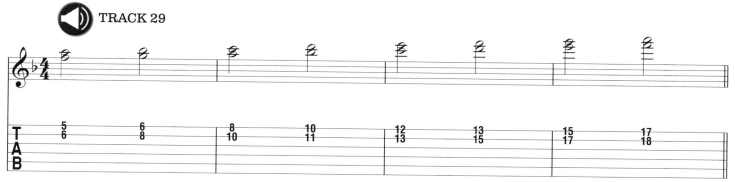

In something a bit more sensitive, here's that same 3rds walk-up with bends on the B string. Throughout the phrase, you'll notice a mixture of half- and whole-step bends. These are used to keep the notes within the F major scale, so you're always bending from a scale tone. Constantly refer to the sound of the fret positions to keep your bends in tune.

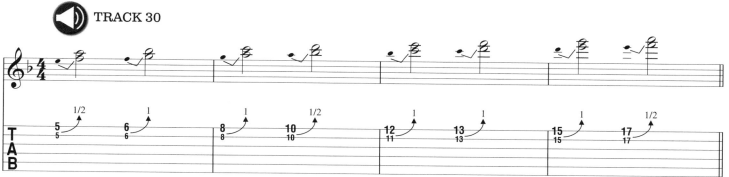

To add a little more melodicism, here's a sequential descent of that same 3rds-in-F major idea. The slides allow you to keep the same finger assignments for bending and fretting. For bending, you get more power when using your third finger, but I've seen positive results using the second; either way, endeavor to develop sensitivity with both fingers.

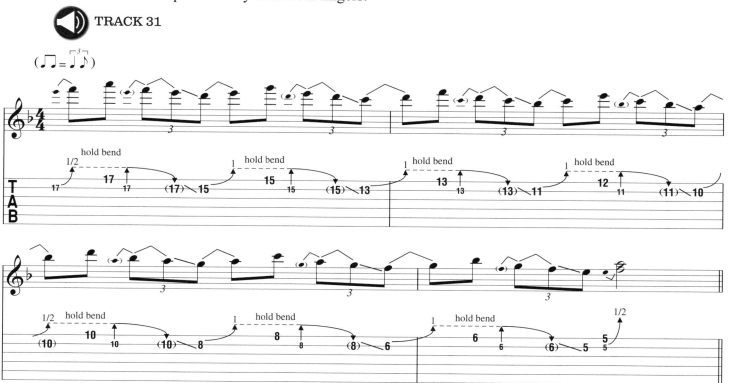

With your fingers and ears in shape, let's apply these moves to an E7 chord. Below are the four available bends on the B and E strings that correspond to the tones of E7 before they start repeating. The intervals between the staves are there to show you the bent/fretted notes respective to the E7 chord. For example, the first double-stop bend shows a 3rd/5th in between the staves; the whole-step bend on the seventh fret, B string yields a G♯ note (3rd of E7), and the seventh fret, E string is a B note (5th of E7).

TRACK 32

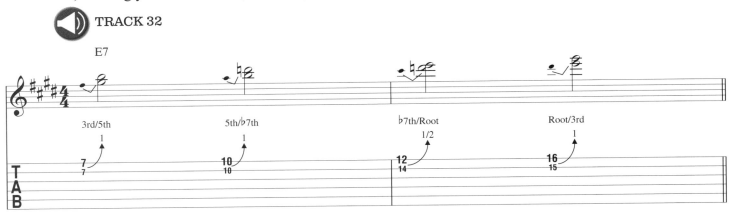

As you can see, the top note of each double stop becomes the bottom note of the next. Try to visualize the underlying chord shape as you bend. For example, the seventh-position, A-form E barre chord has the same top two notes as the 3rd/5th double-stop bend.

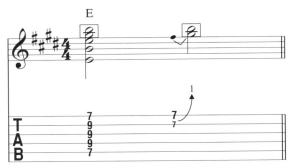

Here are those double-stop bends applied to an uptempo country groove. Hybrid picking these double stops is tricky at this tempo, so you may need to change your approach. After popping the initial double stop, use a lighter touch on the eighth notes, as that'll enhance the staccato sound and create contrast for the accented position shifts.

TRACK 33

Double-stop bends are possible on the G and B strings as well, but not all are practical. The last bend of this example is unique, as it's on the D and G strings and the higher note is bent. Pull the string towards the floor to let the D note at the 12th fret ring.

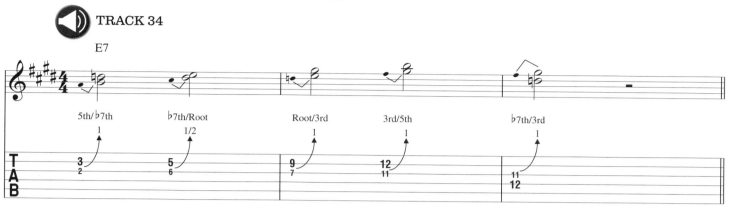

TRACK 34

To bring all the bends together into a usable, close-knit blueprint from which to build your lines, here's a consolidated layout of the most-used double-stop bends. Hopefully these positions and their intervallic functions spark connections in your brain to make them easier to transpose to all keys—especially A, D, and G.

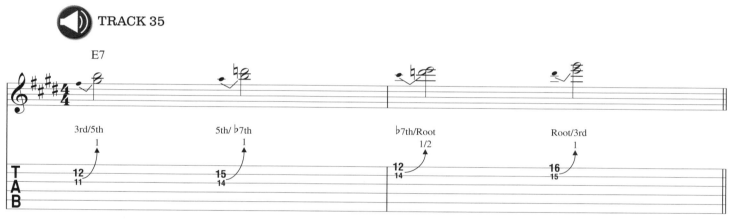

TRACK 35

Here's a lick utilizing that framework in a challenging four-measure phrase. Listen to where the E major and minor pentatonic scales are used.

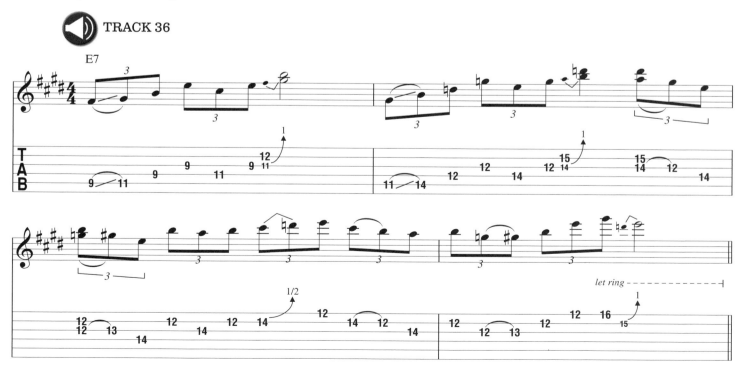

TRACK 36

In this example, you'll hear the effective use of *pre-bends* (bending a string to pitch before picking it) to create a descending G7 line. Measure 2, beat 4 has a challenging move in which three notes ring together (G/F/B). To help with this, pull the G string towards the floor.

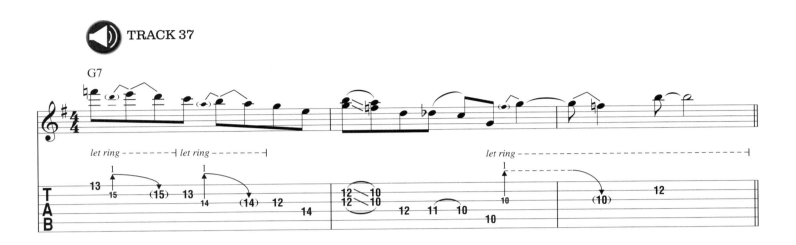

Our pedal steel emulation has brought us through double stops in 3rds, but to expand our repertoire a bit wider, we venture into the world of 6ths. These have the same note spelling as 3rds, but their notes are inverted (i.e., top note becomes bottom, and vice versa).

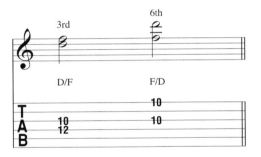

Within the realm of pedal steel licks, these four locations are the most utilized for bending, as the lower string sets are harder to stretch. Again, the intervals between staves represent the bent/fretted notes.

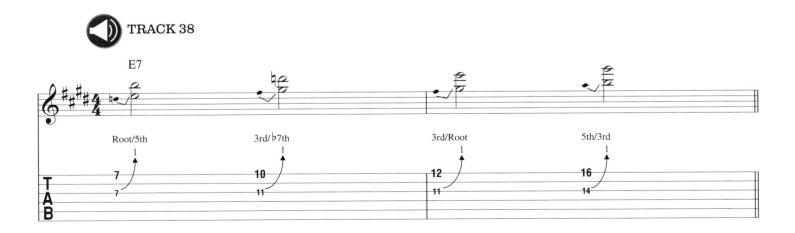

Depending on how and when you bend these shapes, you can imply interesting harmonic movement.

TRACK 39

Those bends are typically done when bending *into* the chord tones. But pre-bends come in handy when you're already grabbing a harmony friendly shape and you release into it. Here are some of the more common pedal steel-like releases for your experimentation. This time, the intervals in between the staves refer to the starting pitch (pre-bend) and the release—e.g., "6th to 5th" is the bent C♯ note being released to B). Note how the 9th-to-root move has two possible top notes; depending on how and where you plot your fingers, the variations with which to create your harmonies are endless.

TRACK 40

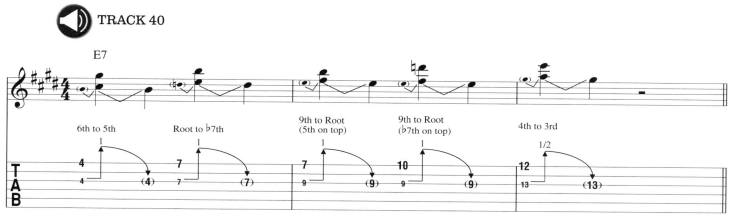

And here's a simple, melodic idea utilizing half- and whole-step bends along with pull-offs to get across a longing quality of mechanical sustain that is the pedal steel.

TRACK 41

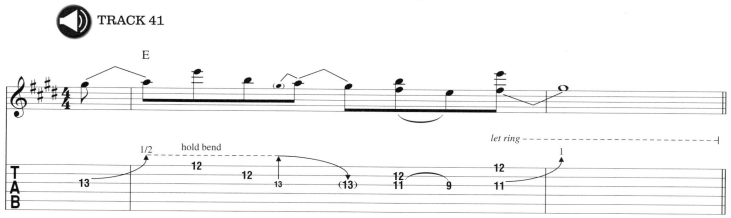

As seen in the previous example, bends aren't your only tool to create pedal steel lines; hammer-ons, pull-offs, slides, and any other techniques that fall comfortably under your hands are at your disposal to get the illusion across. Harmonies, with moving inner and outer voices, are the backbone of the emulation, so follow the forefathers' example and find the *sound* that hearkens back to the pedal steel's mechanical sustain.

Mechanical Benders

Along the lines of guitarists emulating pedal steel sounds, luthiers have taken things a step further to engineer and integrate mechanical benders into their guitars. The brainchild of Clarence White, and fully realized with the help of Gene Parsons, mechanical benders allow physically impossible pedal steel licks to be effortlessly performed on the guitar. Activated by either pulling down or pushing out on the guitar neck, the player has the ability to bend the strings with less effort and greater sustain through the installed bending mechanism routed within the guitar's body.

Connected to the strap button through a complex array of metal fulcrums, a lever pulls on the specific bridge piece (controlling the G or B strings), tightening the string to its tune-able pitch (commonly a whole step). Unfortunately, the installation of the original Parsons-White Bender added 3 or 4 lbs. to the guitar's overall weight, so design re-tools were inevitable.

In the late '80s and early '90s, luthiers like Joe Glaser and Charlie McVay designed less obtrusive models that benefited from modern techniques involving minimal routing and lighter metal parts. These innovations added little more than a pound to the guitar, saving the backs of countless musicians. They also allowed for multiple benders to be installed into a single guitar. Jimmy Olander of Diamond Rio has created a signature sound for the band with his prominent use of double-benders on the G and B strings for hit songs like "Meet in the Middle," "Norma Jean Riley," and "Love a Little Stronger."

OPEN STRINGS

Commonly used to emulate the drones of violin-style lines and to create minor or major 2nd intervals against fretted notes, the juxtaposition of ringing open strings with the rounder sound of fretted notes allows for easier execution of pedal-point ideas and faster legato lines. Getting the most out of this technique may require a little more fretboard knowledge than before, so take it slowly and trust your ears.

One of the more common uses of open strings is to simply replace fretted notes you'd normally play in a scale-like fashion. Here, we have a cool E Mixolydian line that utilizes chromatic notes and slides in an Albert Lee-style descent. With hybrid picking and compression, we get a line full of twang and country flavor.

TRACK 42

But what happens when we replace as many notes as we can with open strings? What was once a line centered around staccato alternate picking becomes a harp-like experience where almost every note rings together, courtesy of hybrid picking and careful finger-arching. With a little note rearranging, minor 2nds like B and B♭, G and G♯, and B♭ and A freely ring into one another because of the open strings.

TRACK 43

This next bluesy, three-measure phrase in E speedily plucks its way through multiple positions with the open E string acting as a drone. Chromatically hammering, pulling, and sliding through the Mixolydian mode, each slur is clawed with the open string to create a gradually closer intervallic relationship with each fretted note through its descent. Measure 1 hammers into the 5th and plucks the 3rd for an easy matter of clawing the adjacent B and E strings simultaneously. Measures 2 and 3 pluck unisons and slide into 2nds for a "timbre-iffic" onslaught of sound, but that comes in tandem with a technical trip-up. Beat 1 of measures 2 and 3, and the "and" of beat 3 in measure 2, have simultaneous plucks of the G and E strings, so practice spreading your second and third fingers a little farther to catch these dyads at speed.

TRACK 44

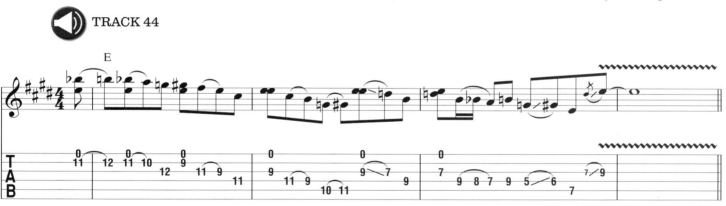

The pedal point quality of open strings was first fully exploited by Ray Flacke when he pulled off fretted diatonic 3rd shapes (sounded melodically, not harmonically) to open strings for a quick and easier-than-it-sounds ascent. Built from the E Mixolydian mode, this example starts on the E/G♯ double stop and chromatically climbs from second to fourth position while pulling off to the G string in a three-against-four rhythm.

TRACK 45

Bringing together the idea of using open strings as note replacements, drones, and avenues for speed, Brad Paisley took inspiration from Eddie Van Halen's legato prowess to play pull-offs from high-register pentatonic scales for oblong-sounding musical phrases.

Our next example, inspired by the opening lick from "Nervous Breakdown," is a descending, open-string pull-off sequence based in the third position G minor pentatonic. In measure 1, the relationship between the fretted notes and the open strings yields minor 2nds (E and F, B and C, respectively), while measure 2 drones G and D notes with fretted and open-string equivalents. Measure 3 continues to exploit these relationships, resulting in quirky minor 3rd and major 6th interval jumps before giving way to chromatically descending pedal points in measure 4 for a bluegrass-inspired tag.

 TRACK 46

Moving the open-string pull-off concept to higher places on the neck creates wider intervals between fretted and open strings, so strategic open-string placement is crucial for creating this melodic hook reminiscent of "Cluster Pluck."

 TRACK 47

DOUBLE-STOP BENDS

Requiring quite a bit more sensitivity and left-hand strength are *double-stop bends*, in which you bend both notes to varying intervals. These are almost exclusively done on the G and B strings, as those strings provide lower tension while the pushing motion of the bend has the leverage needed to make them practical on those strings. Depending on the quality of the dyad that you grab (major or minor), you'll bend it in different ways. Also, intonation of these bends is a matter of musical memory, so as you did with pedal steel bends, check yourself with the intended fretted notes.

Here we have a *major 3rd* dyad (i.e., D and F#). It can easily be recognized as two notes on the same fret of the G and B strings. With this dyad, we'll bend the bottom note a whole step and the top note a half step (D to E, F# to G). Fretting the G and B strings with your third and fourth fingers, respectively, will allow the movement of your wrist to do all the necessary work to keep the notes in pitch.

TRACK 48

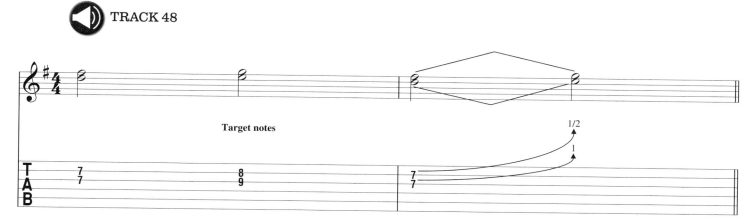

For a *minor 3rd* dyad (i.e., D and F♮), we'll bend each note of the shape a whole step. Because it's necessary to use your second and third fingers for this bend, it's quite a bit more challenging, as you only have your first finger to provide the extra bending help. This is where your developed wrist action is taxed the most, so push carefully.

TRACK 49

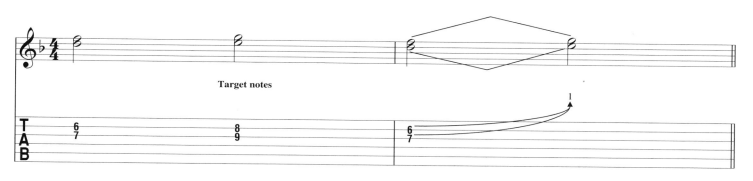

Once you can play these bends by feel, ear-twisting ideas like this one can enhance your solos and fills. We first bend both notes of the minor 3rd shape, but playing them individually gives a further illusion of pedal steel mechanics being at work.

TRACK 50

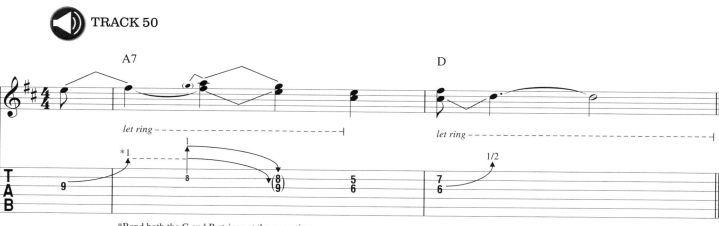

*Bend both the G and B strings at the same time.

Sustaining these bends in pitch while playing surrounding notes is yet another tricky facet of the technique's complexity. Further emulating pedal steel sounds is our next example in A, inspired by Jerry Donahue's version of "The Claw." Starting with a bend from the major 3rd shape to the 5th/♭7th (E/G) of A, this slow blues lick uses pull-offs to open strings and double stops from the minor pentatonic and ends with an oblique bend of the 3rd/5th (C♯/E) after a quick position shift. The E-string pull-off will expose out-of-tune bends, so get the lick in your ears with the fretted equivalents if you're having trouble.

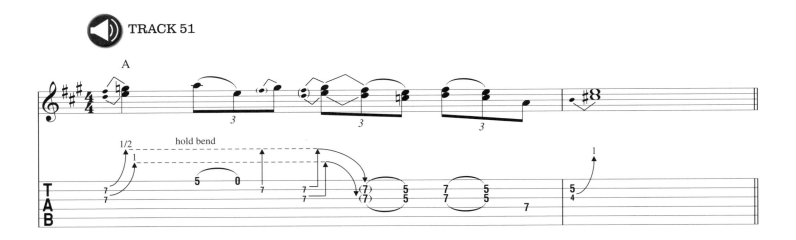

TRACK 51

It's also possible to imply harmonic movement with these bends if you time it right. The first two beats of the next example will challenge your hands and ears with the minor 3rd double-stop bend to the 3rd/5th of C (E/G) while sustaining the root on the E string during the bend's release. Bend with your third and second finger on the G and B strings, respectively, but make sure the bend stays in pitch as you hold down the E string with your fourth finger. The rest of the pedal steel-style line is a matter of strategic finger placement for ultimate sustain, so keep the second and third fingers planted on the G and B strings as you use the first finger and fourth fingers for E and D strings, respectively.

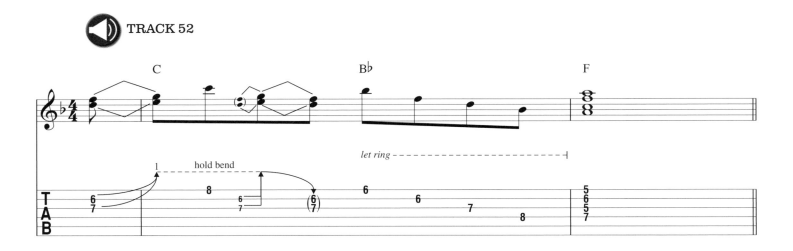

TRACK 52

BEHIND-THE-NUT BENDS

Because of the fixed bridge and the recessed headstock design of the Telecaster, *behind-the-nut bends* have become a favorite since Jerry Donahue explored the ringing and harmonic possibilities of the technique. Playing these bends will test your calluses, so explore the nether regions of your fretboard with care.

The methods for developing bending sensitivity behind the nut are the same as those for developing them on the fretboard: use your ears and reference the intended notes. To perform this technique safely, take your second finger, reinforced by your first, and push down on the string about 1/4-inch behind the nut. Closer than that, there isn't enough length on either side of the string to push down at least a whole step. Because of this, strings 5–2 are the most easily utilized, while the surrounding strings are less opportunistic.

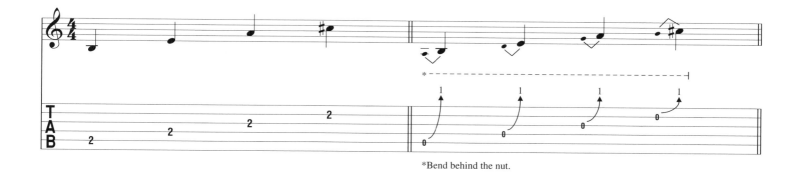

*Bend behind the nut.

With these parameters in mind and the fact that half-step bends are harder to feel, not many notes are available (B, E, A, and C♯), but the opportunities are limited to your chord theory and melodic awareness. For melodic applications, tired G major pentatonic lines are given a unique timbre when bent from behind the nut. Bending in rhythm and in pitch is always a challenge, so referencing the fretted equivalents is encouraged.

TRACK 53

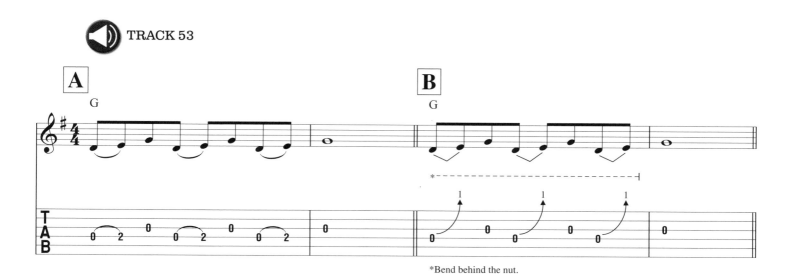

*Bend behind the nut.

Behind-the-nut bends are effective when bending into the chord tones to punctuate the end of a phrase. In the following lick, take advantage of not having to fret the open-A string when shifting your hand back to position in time for the bend.

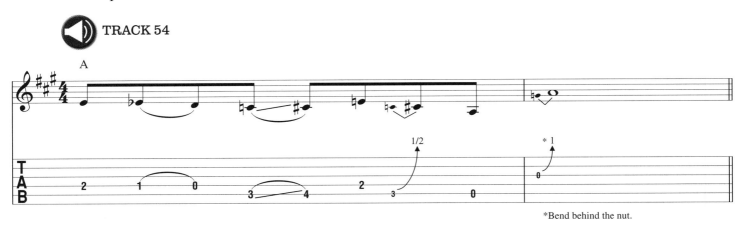

TRACK 54

*Bend behind the nut.

More difficult are those utilizing fretted notes *and* behind-the-nut bends. Here, grab the first fret, B string with your pinky and use the bend's release to grab the third fret, D string in time.

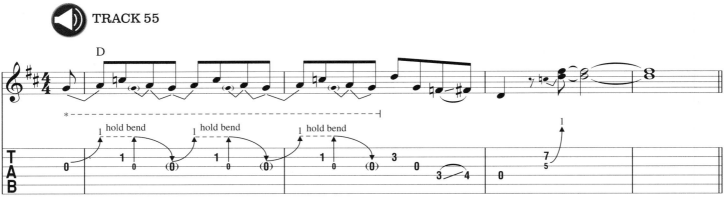

TRACK 55

*Bend behind the nut.

CHAPTER 4: COUNTRIFY YOUR LICKS

Every guitarist is initially exposed to either rock or blues phrases when their desire to solo strikes. The appeal of the technical flash and sound of the distorted guitar is irresistible to the budding rock star, and the licks perfectly expand their basic pentatonic knowledge. When the interest for learning country strikes, some feel that they need to throw away their old licks and learn new ones from scratch to become authentic pickers.

Fear not. As a sort of stylistic comparison, in this section, we're going to morph standard rock vocabulary into country phrases. Licks you already know can be tweaked in ways to make them sing and twang with the best of them. Taking what we know from the licks we learned in the previous chapter, we can glean a few "Do's and Don'ts" to enhance or limit our lines.

1. TURN OFF THE DISTORTION

Most of the sustain in rock soloing comes from distortion. You can hear it in the constant use of pinch harmonics, rapid-fire legato runs, tapping, and held bends with wide vibrato. Here's a repeating, hard rock riff in E minor pentatonic. The intent of the line is more for the legato, "sheets of sound" effect, afforded by saxophone-inspired distortion and vibrato-laden bends.

TRACK 56

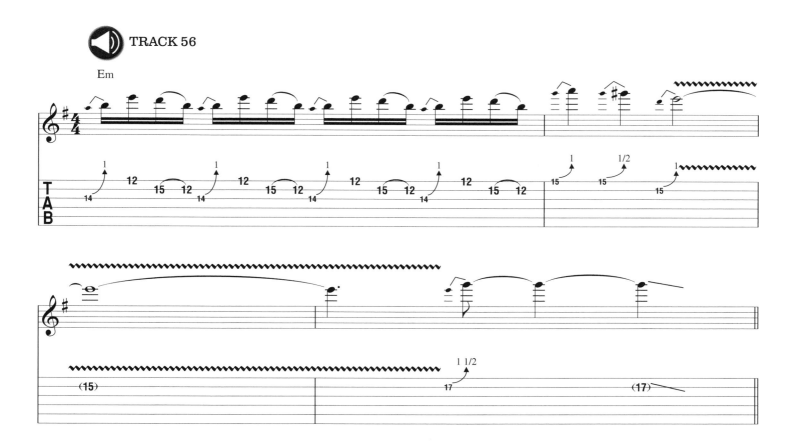

Trading distortion for compression forces us to limit our repeating legato lick and forego held notes. Poised to replace the intrigue of distortion's sustain are hammer-ons, pull-offs, slides, and fret-hand muting to create unexpected rhythmic accents. By using the repeating minor pentatonic motive as a starting point, we can create a bluesy, Mixolydian-flavored melodic descent. The variety of double stops, scales, and articulations creates something uniquely country with equal amounts of melody and technical challenge.

TRACK 57

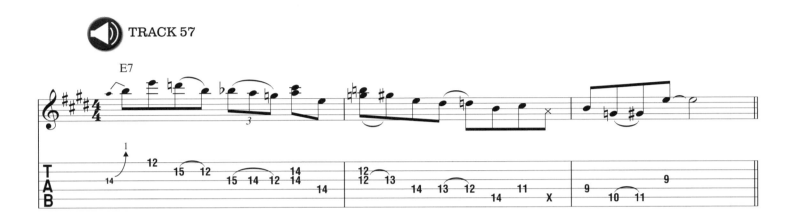

While the overtones generated by distortion coupled with amplifier feedback is a wonderful cacophony of sound when it's controlled at a rock concert, the over-the-top pyrotechnics of Jimi Hendrix are not fitting when you're sharing the stage with singers inspired by the heartfelt subtlety of country music's founding father, Hank Williams. Intelligent note choice and precise articulation are the hallmarks of country guitar, and they can't be expressed with obscene amounts of gain.

2. USE DOUBLE STOPS AND OPEN STRINGS

You lose harmony and timbre with distortion, so capitalize on the subtlety and effectiveness of open strings and double stops, now that compression provides the clean sustain. Here's an A minor pentatonic phrase out of the standard blues vocabulary.

TRACK 58

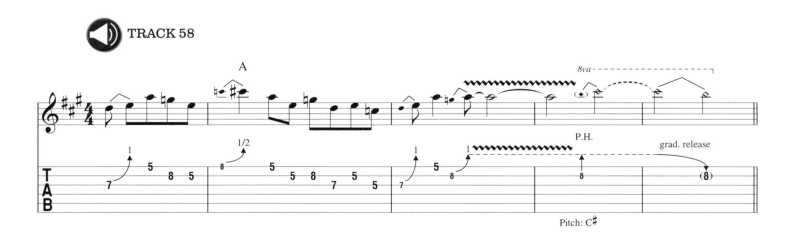

And here's that phrase morphed into a Brent Mason-style lick with double stops and open strings. The pickup measure ultimately remains the same, but substituting the open E string for the fifth fret, B string allows for easier position shifting. In measure 1, we replace the half-step C# bend with an A/C# double stop, eschewing the blues cliché by sliding up to the ninth position for a double-stop descent through the A Mixolydian mode with triplet pull-offs in between. As you can hear, the A/C# (root/3rd of A7) and G/B (♭7th/9th of A7) double stops create harmonic interest, while the triplet pull-offs and slides add rhythmic motion and unpredictability to the phrase.

TRACK 59

3. CHANGE YOUR SOLOING POINTS OF REFERENCE

As you can see and hear from the previous lick transformations, country sensibilities effortlessly add chromaticism and rhythmic surprises to rock lines. This is possible because there is a crucial difference between how rock and country players visualize the fretboard. While rock players typically rely on pentatonic and blues scale shapes as their points of reference, country musicians primarily visualize chord positions, connect those to the scale shapes they already know, and build licks that fluidly connect those positions. To make the line sound convincing, the chord tones almost always land on the beat, so players design their chromaticism and passing tones around those points, depending on the underlying feel of the song.

Let's start off with a lick for a G7 chord. Here are the positions we'll be using, which span from seventh to open position. They voice-lead pretty well into each other and, once learned, are great places to get your bearings as they all connect to familiar G major and minor pentatonic scale shapes.

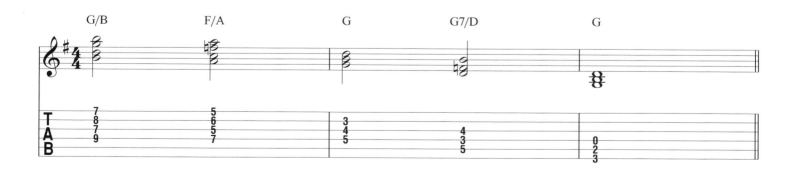

The first two chords in the above example (G/B and F/A) are important to dwell on for a bit. While they're both *first inversion chords* (the 3rd is in the bass), they're still G and F chords. To create a Mixolydian sound, you can play triads based on the root and ♭7th, also known as the *whole-step down approach*. You can also play the chromatic notes in between those shapes, because they are the ♭3rd and ♭5th from the funky-sounding blues scale and the ♮7th from the G major scale.

Here's an interesting swung G7 line that connects those positions in two-measure phrases. In measure 1, the G/B and F/A positions have similar chromatic pull-off lines. Measure 2 applies the chromatic elements from our whole-step down approach for a Jerry Reed-style descent in double stops. A D♭/F double-stop bend begins measure 3 for a major/minor pentatonic line at the third position, and we end in open position, courtesy of slides and pull-offs.

TRACK 60

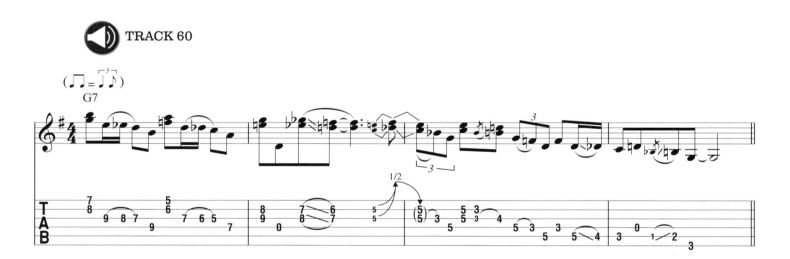

In the next chapter, we'll delve deeper into the various scales that country musicians use, but the whole-step down approach and chord tone soloing should be at the back of your mind as you countrify your licks.

4. ANTICIPATE STRONG BEATS

Building on our double stops, open strings, and budding chromatic awareness, sliding, slurring, and bending into strong beats infuses jazz sophistication into our country phrasing. This not only de-emphasizes the strong beats, it also opens opportunities for creating Latin-style rhythms that accent the offbeats.

This I–vi–II–V jazz turnaround melodically connects seventh arpeggios with chromatically descending voice leading while consistently slurring into beats 1 and 3 for a swing-inspired line. The diminished arpeggios are particularly striking in their application, as they serve an interesting function in the chromatic descent by implying ♭9th extensions to sell the harmonic sophistication.

TRACK 61

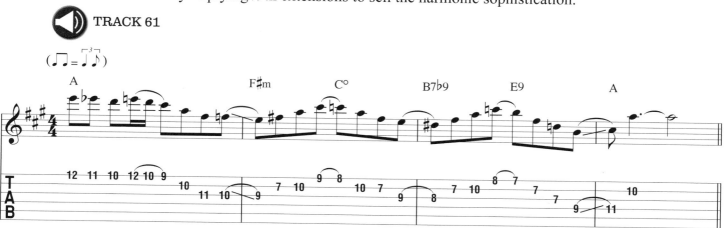

To apply some of these phrasing concepts to a country context, we'll replace the diminished harmony with double stops and open strings from the Mixolydian mode while retaining the melodicism and slurred phrasing of jazz.

TRACK 62

De-emphasizing strong beats by sliding and slurring into them isn't the only interesting way to create forward rhythmic motion. Accenting the offbeats with 16th notes (or faster) just prior to the strong beat adds technical challenge as well as interest. Here's a rhythmic blueprint to construct your line from that treats beats 2 and 4 as strong beats.

From that blueprint, we've written a minor pentatonic/Mixolydian lick in E that starts by bending into a G♯/B double stop on the "and" of beat 4. This anticipation displaces the expected accents and gives way for the interest that ensues with the slurring 16th-note rhythms. Using double stops on the "and" of beat 2 and beat 3 with the 16th notes lends a surprising twist of accents that helps make the slurs sound as though they're coming out of nowhere (which is the effect we're going for!).

TRACK 63

CHAPTER 5: PROGRESSION ANALYSIS

Before any notes of a solo are to be played, the full gamut of harmonic possibilities of a given chord progression should be understood and internalized, as most players' ear-to-hands connection is not instantaneous for off-the-cuff improvisation. With the easy-to-read Nashville Number System, we'll determine the appropriate scale and melodic devices to play, and the right time for them, in the 16-bar blues for which we'll be writing a solo in Chapter 6. The analysis process, along with the concepts we employ in this chapter, should be regular prep for any solo you write in your formative efforts.

This chapter also endeavors to widen our sonic palette and expand our harmonic awareness as a solid foundation for playing solos with wider thematic ideas. The musically theoretical subject matter is of an advanced nature where fretboard familiarity is a pre-requisite, so minimal review will be offered.

NASHVILLE NUMBER SYSTEM

The *Nashville Number System* is a shorthand for quickly writing out chord progressions and even single-note lines in which Arabic numerals and other symbols represent the intervals of an established key. Developed by the Jordanaires to map out their complicated four-part harmonies in the heat of the studio while singing for Elvis Presley, the Nashville Number System's use of numbers instead of note names allowed songs to be transcribed and even transposed from one key to another very quickly. Many books describing the varied symbols and intricacies of the system have been written, but the principles applicable to our purposes are twofold: what the numbers mean and how the page is set up.

The numbers of the system represent intervals of the major scale. For the C major scale that consists of the scale tones C–D–E–F–G–A–B, the numbers would simply become 1–2–3–4–5–6–7. Simple enough? Well, to go a little deeper, we can modify the numbers to create modes and other scales. Can you guess what the number sequence 1–2–3–4–5–6–♭**7** makes up? That would be the Mixolydian mode! (The most common scale used in country music.)

To write out a C, F, and G chord progression, you'd normally see something as cumbersome as this:

At first glance, it's tricky to see what we need to play because of the layout. But on closer inspection, we find that there are four measures of C and two measures of F and G. Most arrangers want to fit as many measures into one system as possible, so the layout can get tight and more confusing to follow than it needs to be.

Here's that same progression written out in the Nashville Number System. First, we need to establish which key the numbers will be referencing, so we write "Key of C" at the top of the page. Since most country music is in 4/4 time, we can assume that's what this progression is in, but *compound meters* (i.e., 3/4, 6/8, 12/8, etc.) should be noted. Each number represents one measure of 4/4 time, so you'd play the "1" chord for four measures, the "4" chord for two measures, and so on.

This simplified presentation of the same information is valuable in many ways: it takes up less space, it's easily transposable, and it's instantly readable. But other than exposing you to the requisite knowledge of Nashville studio playing, this system of writing out your charts allows you to think in four-measure chunks. This way of thinking will help give your solos more of a dynamic ebb and flow and aid our progression analysis when deciding what scales, arpeggios, and licks we use and when.

SCALES

With roots in blues, rock, and even jazz, country guitar soloing has become a mix of pentatonic, modal, and arpeggio-based approaches for its simple yet sophisticated sound.

The following scale shapes will be respective to the key of A at the fifth position, throughout, for easier transposition. Remember that the notes of the A7 chord are A, C♯, E, and G (root, 3rd, 5th, and ♭7th); how these notes relate to the scale tones available from each shape is important to how lines are constructed, so keep them in mind.

The most basic of the scales is the *major pentatonic scale*. Consisting of five notes (*penta* meaning "five"), the major pentatonic scale adds the 2nd and 6th intervals to a major triad, seen as B and F♯ in A major. The 2nd and 6th intervals accentuate the major quality of the triad as these are its most common extensions, more frequently seen as the *9th* and *13th* (same notes as the 2nd and 6th, but an octave higher).

A Major Pentatonic Scale

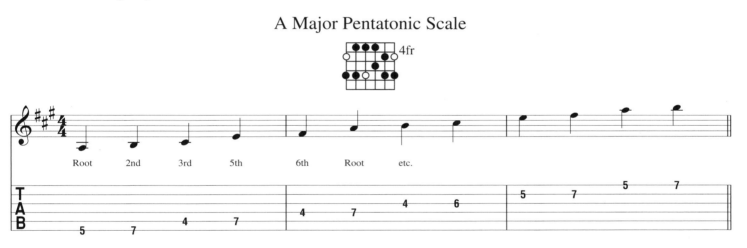

The more commonly known scale is the *minor pentatonic scale*. The formula of arguably the first scale all guitarists learn is built from a *minor seventh arpeggio* (Root–♭3rd–5th–♭7th) with a 4th passing tone. Along with its obvious applications to playing in minor keys, here's where most of the chromatic notes surrounding the dominant seventh arpeggio come into play.

A Minor Pentatonic Scale

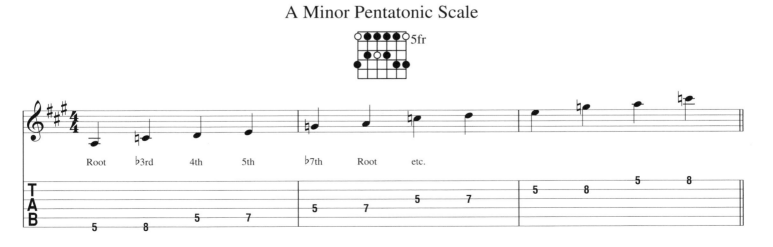

Adding a ♯4th/♭5th interval to the minor pentatonic gives us the *blues scale*, chromatically connecting the whole step between the 4th and 5th scale degrees.

A Blues Scale

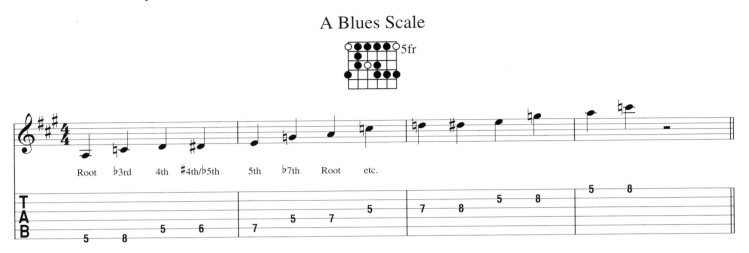

When you consider these available notes while remembering the underlying triads as target notes, you'll begin to see from where the chromaticism and double stops in country music are derived. To start out, here we have an A7 arpeggio in quarter notes.

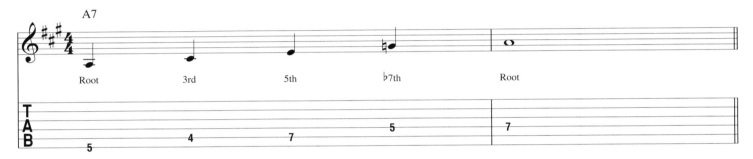

To make things a bit more interesting, we're going to use notes from each of the aforementioned scales as approach tones for the A7 arpeggio: the ♭7th, ♭3rd, and the ♭5th from the blues scale are used as approach tones for the A, C♯, and E notes, respectively, while the 6th (F♯) from the major pentatonic scale approaches the ♭7th (G). This creates a cleverly chromatic, pedal steel-style line that perfectly plots the chord tones on the beat.

TRACK 64

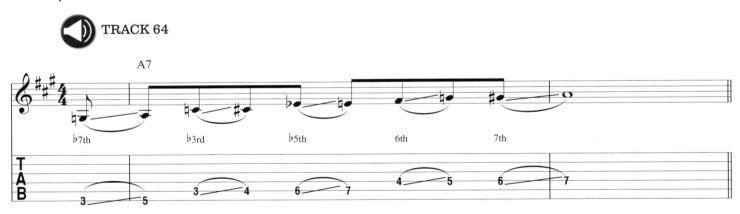

While this is a great exercise in the thought process behind *chord-tone soloing*, thinking in this type of scale minutiae can get quite overwhelming when you're starting out and want your ideas to flow. (That A7 idea is basically approaching each chord tone from a half step below, and only after analyzing it did I discover the connections between the passing tones and the scales themselves.) Referring chromatic notes back to separate scales is counter-productive to the uninitiated ear and against the sound-mixing quality of country lines. To get the most out of these notes, let's organize them in a more meaningful way.

Aside from the A7 arpeggio, the notes available from the major pentatonic, the minor pentatonic, and the blues scale are: 2nd, ♭3rd, 4th, ♯4th/♭5th, and 6th. When you combine all these notes into a useful shape, you get a hybrid scale called the *Mixolydian-blues scale*. This "super scale" has just about all the chromatic notes you'll need for country's spanky sound. These passing notes mean that all the chromatic notes between the 2nd and 5th are available, opening a lot of interesting possibilities when you apply the Mixolydian-blues scale to all the 1–4–5 chords of a typical country song.

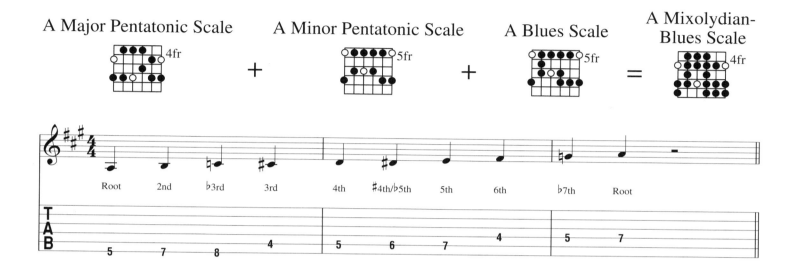

Seeing this scale as a combination of major and minor pentatonics plus the blues scale isn't the only meaningful connection to theory. It's also the *Mixolydian mode* (Root, 2nd, 3rd, 4th, 5th, 6th, ♭7th) plus two passing notes from the blues scale: the ♭3rd and the ♯4th/♭5th. It's interesting to think that combining common pentatonic scales can shed new light on a seemingly complex mode. As you can see, studying music from an intervallic perspective demonstrates the truly interconnected elements of theory and helps solidify ideas while opening up musical complexities for all to understand.

With our available scales well in hand, writing lines that freely mix major, minor, Mixolydian, and blues sounds (i.e., using the Mixolydian-blues scale) within a complete phrase is the hallmark of country soloing. Here we have a four-measure A7 line featuring all those ingredients with double stops, repeated riffs, and chromaticism.

TRACK 65

Knowing scales all over the neck affords the ability to transpose ideas to other keys.

TRACK 66

Recognizing the arpeggios, notes, and scales available within a given position allows you to subtly change the notes of your phrase to work with an upcoming chord. It may take some practice to be able to do it off the cuff, but it's worth the time and effort to have that kind of instant fluidity in your playing.

TRACK 67

TRANSITIONAL LICKS

In order to smoothly and logically navigate a 16-bar blues, we'll need to learn how to analyze chord progressions, as the relationships between our current and destination chords are unique and creating harmonic motion towards them is crucial for the proper country sophistication. Because of the simplistic structure of the blues, the ways a chord can be addressed are pretty loose, but the strongest resolution in harmony is by addressing the chord's 3rd (be it major or minor), so we'll have it as our focal point.

So how do we strongly address the 3rd of a given chord? Well, one of the best ways is through a jazz approach called *chromatic approach patterns*. Here we have the E Mixolydian-blues scale with the notes from F♯ to B bracketed, because they're all half steps. By carefully plotting E chord tones on the beat, we can use these notes in ways to strongly address the 3rd by forming chromatic approach patterns.

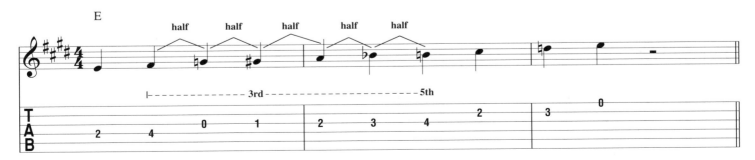

Here, we have a chromatic approach pattern in E that descends from three half steps above (5th to 4th) and approaches the 3rd from one below (♭3rd). Variation A inverts the chromatic pattern by starting on the 4th and ascending to the 5th before approaching from a half step below. Variation B replaces the ♭3rd with the 2nd, approaching the 3rd via a scale step.

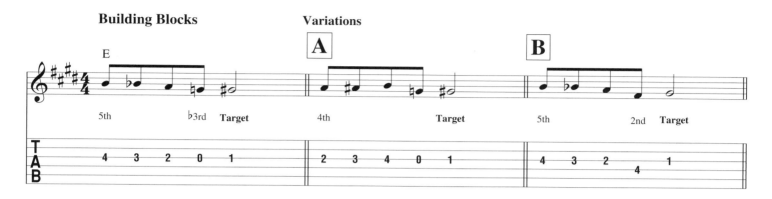

Utilizing 3rd shapes to flesh out and disguise the literal chromaticism brings slippery freshness and unexpected accents to the goal of addressing the major 3rd of E (G♯).

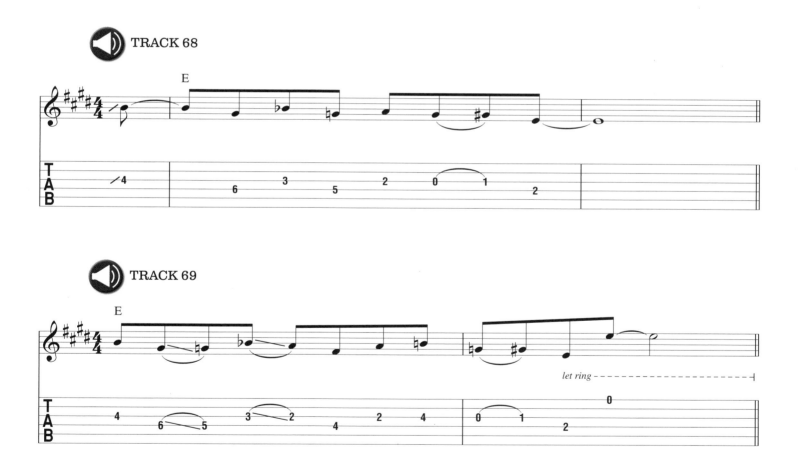

These patterns also work for approaching the 5th and ♭7th, as well, so experiment with the chromatic and scale-step approach patterns to find what sounds good to you.

Now that we have an idea of how to effectively address the 3rd via chromatic approach patterns, the first step in our analysis is to convert our progression to the Nashville Number System, so the intervallic connections are more obvious and become theoretically universal.

Our progression in E:			becomes...

Our progression in E:				Key of E			
E	E	E	E	1	1	1	1
A	A	E	E	4	4	1	1
B	B	A	A	5	5	4	4
E	E	E	E	1	1	1	1

After looking at the number chart, we can easily see that there are four sets of harmonic motion:

- *1 chord to the 4 chord*

- *4 chord to the 1 chord*

- *1 chord to the 5 chord*

- *5 chord to the 4 chord*

The musical function behind each of these resolutions is unique, and we'll itemize each. While the best target note that yields the strongest resolution is always the chord's 3rd, preparing the listener for that resolution is where careful line construction is needed.

1 CHORD TO THE 4 CHORD

The secret behind this line is by implying the ♭7th of the 1, because it resolves by a half step to the 3rd of the 4 chord. For the key of E, the ♭7th of 1 is D, and the 3rd of the 4 chord (A) is C♯. Here's a skeleton of our chromatic approach pattern.

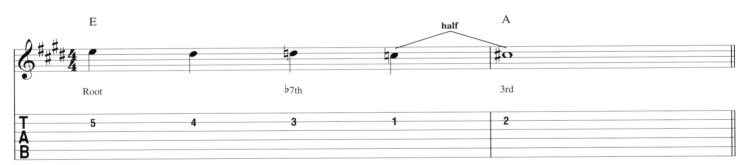

Fleshing it out with double stops, slides, and open strings lends the sought-after country flavor to an otherwise jazzy concept.

TRACK 70

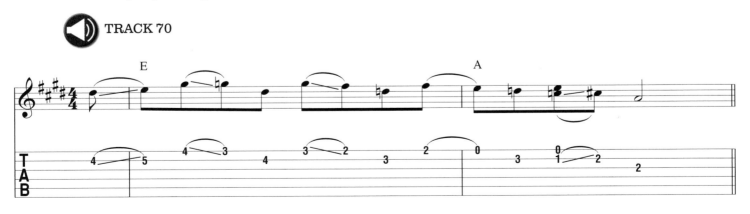

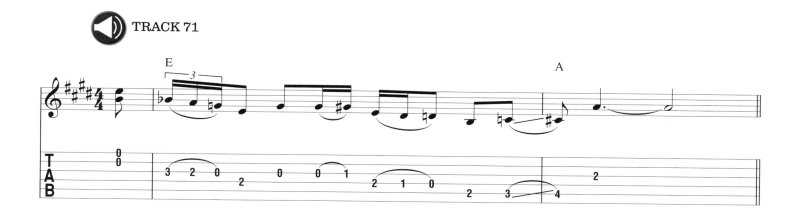

4 CHORD TO THE 1 CHORD & 1 CHORD TO THE 5 CHORD

Interestingly, both of these changes resolve to the next chord by moving up a 5th interval. In the key of E, E is the 5th of A (**A**, **C♯**, **E: Root**, **3rd**, **5th**), and B is the 5th of E (**E**, **G♯**, **B**). For each chord, the ♭7th is only a half step away from the following chord's 3rd, which is perfect for repeating riffs like these that take advantage of smooth voice leading and rhythmic displacement.

TRACK 72

TRACK 73

Notice how well the lines flow into the next chord? Careful plotting of your licks will transform your solos into an overall cohesive statement rather than an avenue for you to show off your best licks in a forced, disjointed sequence of rehearsed desperation.

5 CHORD TO THE 4 CHORD

This change is unique in that these chords are a whole step apart, which is the perfect opportunity for playing similar licks for each. This triplet-based lick in B climbs the fourth-position major pentatonic and descends the Mixolydian-blues scale to address the 3rd (D♯) via chromatic approach tones from the 5th and finally ends on the root.

TRACK 74

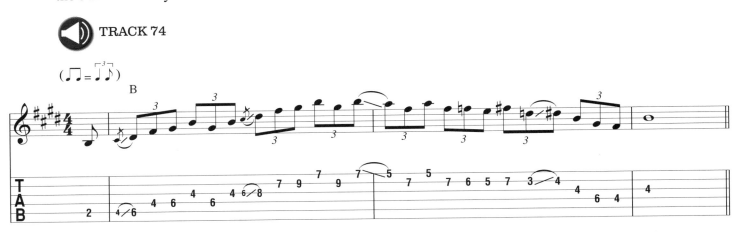

Here, we employ the whole-step down approach to create a transposed lick from B to work over an A chord with the second-position A major pentatonic and Mixolydian-blues scales.

TRACK 75

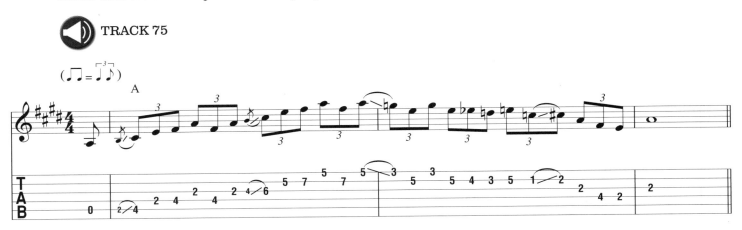

Being the twelfth measure of the solo, this technique is useful for a couple of thematic reasons: it provides rhythmic and harmonic contrast from the dissimilar ideas of the 1–4–1 changes, and maintains melodic continuity so the listener has something to hold on to as a sort of psychological rest in preparation for the climactic final four measures of the solo.

Theory Disclaimer

While these guidelines are specific and detailed, they are by no means conclusive. The creation of music is not mathematic or formulaic, in which the harmonic movement of a 5th interval automatically needs "this" or "that" scale. These ideas should be filtered through your judgment to determine how smoothly each lick flows into the other, the context of the song's groove, and whether the licks sound good or not. The licks you use shouldn't be deemed valid through their intervallic relationship to the chord; in the end, your ears should be the final authority on what to play.

CHAPTER 6: COUNTRIFY YOUR SOLOS

In this last chapter, we'll add a few more theory heavy tricks to our repertoire, and then work through the thought process of creating a complete solo based on a backing track.

DOUBLE STOPS

Despite all the applications of double stops heard in country, the construction of effective double-stop lines is the least understood. Instead of a vertical exercise in 3rd, 4th, and 6th intervals, the most intriguing double-stop riffs are those featuring both melodic and dissonant *voice leading*. A line that weaves in and out, rhythmically pushes the music forward, and excites the listener's musical imagination is our ultimate goal.

A good place to start is by writing a single-note line that already sounds good by itself.

TRACK 76

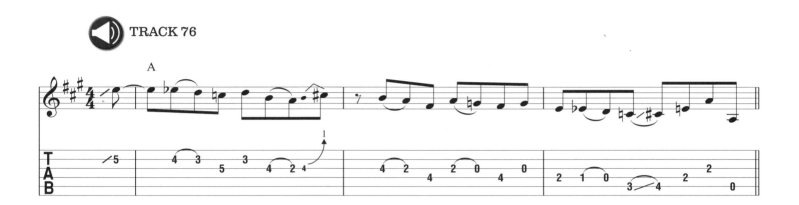

From there, we gradually layer in the top melody of the double stops, hopefully creating voice leading, interval skips, and allowing the single-note lines to smoothly flow from the top and bottom melody notes. In measure 1, the top notes are descending in stepwise motion from the root to the 5th of the A Mixolydian mode (A–G–F#–E). In measure 2, minor 3rd jumps from E to C# break the scale steps only to proceed with a whole-step pull-off to B.

TRACK 77

Another way to look at this is by studying the isolated double stops. Notice how they anticipate the beat and chromatically descend while the top notes sustain with moving notes and utilize a variety of intervals to create harmonic and rhythmic motion.

TRACK 78

Jerry Reed was the master of this technique. Check out his interesting counterpoint melodies using double stops in songs like "Red Hot Picker." While double stops and position-shifting slides abound in measures 1 through 3, this next example utilizes 5ths, tritones, and 3rds in measure 4 to great effect for an ear-twisting top and bottom melody of chromatic counterpoint.

TRACK 79

Taking a nod from Jerry's instrumental and technical masterpiece, "The Claw," the next example features another display of well-placed double stops. The chromatically descending inner line with A pedal points of measure 1 and beyond creates interesting intervals of 4ths, tritones, major 3rds, minor 3rds, and 6ths for a propelling hybrid picking phrase of rhythmic and intervallic intrigue.

TRACK 80

Double stops also work great for descending lines as well. In this next example, notice how the top notes of the 3rds (D, C, and B) are serving as target notes for a chromatically charged blues phrase. Check out how the accents are spread across the measure to see and hear how they propel the line forward.

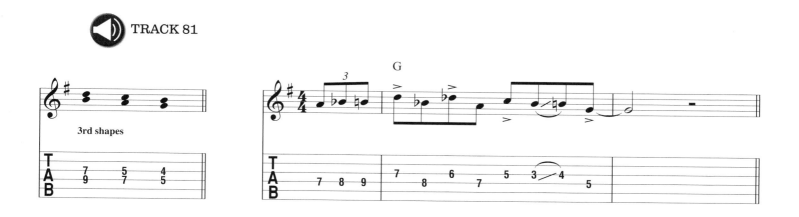

TRACK 81

3rd shapes

REPEATING RIFFS

Expounding on our chord theory and challenging our hybrid picking chops are *repeating riffs*. Another iconic contribution from Jerry Reed, further realized by Brent Mason in solos from "I Don't Even Know Your Name," these ostinato figures coupled with double stops create odd groupings that twist and turn the accents across the measure for a rhythmically syncopated approach to solo construction.

Here we have a five-note repeating riff for a G7 chord, which is basically outlining the arpeggio with double-stop hits to create the accents. Because of its odd, five-note grouping over an even pulse (4/4), it takes three measures for the pattern to rhythmically start on beat 1 again. This change of accents is called a *hemiola*, and it's a very useful device to create tension and continuity because it melodically repeats and rhythmically changes. It also serves as a great building block for your four-measure phrases, because after the idea repeats for the fourth time, all you have to do is play a short idea to close the phrase.

TRACK 82

To enhance this quality of tension while diminishing the continuity, let's change the melodic content of the repeats by moving them through different inversions of G7 in a double-stop descent. In between the staves are the names of the chord shapes (learned in Chapter 4) from which the ideas are built; they're also placed at the points where the tricky position shifts are, so practice those shifts first!

TRACK 83

The most challenging and interesting application of repeating riffs are those that are played over changing chords. Keeping with the idea of playing in four-measure phrases, compensation for the change in harmonic movement is best done by changing one or two notes of the phrase—this is where your chord theory comes in. Below is a progression from A to D. In measures 1 and 2, we have a repeating riff with a G/C♯ double stop (♭7th/3rd of A7) and a repeating F♯–E (6th–5th of A7) ostinato figure in between. To retain the repeating riff over the D chord in measures 3 and 4, we subtly change the G/C♯ double stop to A/C (5th/♭7th of D7). Since the F♯–E figure serves as the 3rd and 2nd of D7, the lick works great while retaining thematic continuity with the repeating riff of the A7 chord.

TRACK 84

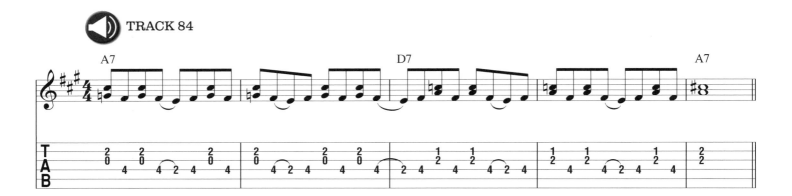

In the previous example, we implied just two chords with the double stops in our repeating riff (A7 and D7). To add a bit more complexity, we can imply the major triads as well to create chromatic voice leading (C, C♯, and D) and step-wise motion for the notes of the ostinato figure (E, F♯, G, and A).

TRACK 85

Playing similar ideas like this over different chords maintains continuity with your lines and retains the listener's interest. Repeating riffs lull the listener into a state of thinking that they can predict your next idea, so following it up with a technical and rhythmic surprise will add climax and points of interest to your solos.

BACKING TRACK

The solo we'll be working on at the end of this chapter will take place over a 16-bar blues backing track. This fun, uptempo, Louisiana-style country-blues in E is not only a challenging groove to solo over, but features a lot of interesting rhythm approaches—a nice break from just strumming away on cowboy chords.

Sliding into a fretted open D-string drone, followed by a snappy triplet pull-off descent through and around an E7 arpeggio to a low E-string bend, the opening riff is a prime example of country surprise and a welcome intro to the backdrop of our soloing adventures.

Providing obvious harmonic interest, the 6th-based boogie patterns of the E and A chords challenge your hybrid picking dexterity—especially in measure 4, where the E7 double stops rhythmically invert to a single-note line that chromatically approaches the A chord.

Measures 9–12 over the B and A chords alternate palm-muted roots and hybrid-picked double stops on the offbeats, but the 4th double stops of the B chord are contrasted with the A's sliding tritone (i.e., G/C♯) move in measure 12. Returning to the E6 boogie pattern in measure 13 for three measures, the proceedings close with the opening riff's E7 pull-off figure that leads into the ensemble hit on beat 2 of the final measure.

TRACK 86

Moderately fast Country ♩ = 172

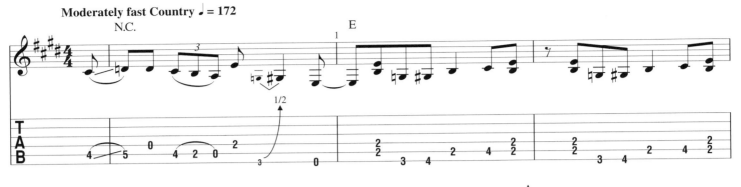

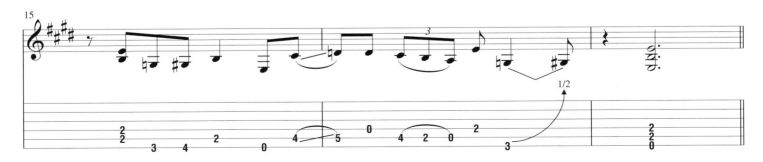

PLOTTING LICKS

Being an effective soloist not only requires advanced technical chops and a seemingly endless well of rhythmically and melodically exciting ideas, a sixth sense of ensemble awareness needs to be cultivated with active listening and then manifested through practice and experimentation of applied musical instinct. The active listening aspect is what we'll concern ourselves with as we plot the flow and contour of the solo we'll play over the backing track.

Having listened, learned, and played the backing track, we can use that groove to discern what to play based on how harmonically and rhythmically busy it is. With pretty much each chord, the ♭7th is played, so a Mixolydian-blues scale approach for note choice would be an obvious fit. There is also quite a bit of rhythmic syncopation in the main riff, as suggested by the accented double stops being played on the "and" of beat 1 and the "and" of beat 4 in each measure, so that can become a recurring theme. Taking all these factors into account helps inform our solo's ebb and flow, and here are my first-impression thoughts on the matter:

MEASURES 1–4

Being the start of the solo, a composed, yet catchy melodic statement in the higher register will contrast well with the opening bass-string lick and give the listener something to hang on to.

MEASURE 5–8

After the melodic descent, a quick, technical ascent through the A chord would effectively cap the first eight measures of the solo.

MEASURES 9–12

Because of the faster, more complex harmonic activity of the rhythm part, another melodically catchy series of two-measure phrases over the B and A chords would work well if they intervallically mirrored each other.

MEASURES 13–16

These last four measures over the E chord should gradually bring down the proceedings with new thematic material that reacts to the ensemble hit in measure 17. Perhaps even play through the quarter-note rest of beat 1 there.

The contrast of the melodic and the technical, ascent and descent, along with repetition and innovation, are all thematic elements a soloist uses to take the listener on a dynamic musical journey. Having a plan for where you want the solo to go and where it can go shapes the thought processes behind the truly iconic solos of all music. This maturity only comes with experience and thoughtful preparation. Put in the extra effort before your moment in the spotlight and move beyond the instinct to mindlessly wail!

SOLO

And finally, here's the solo for you to see how these concepts were applied in real-time. Despite having a clear blueprint with thematic concepts in place, the construction of the melodic and rhythmic ideas was a challenge, so the following analysis is offered.

The first five measures of the solo establish a descending call-and-response motif that utilizes single-note lines between each double-stop anticipation. Over the E chord, the solo opens with a B/D (5th/♭7th) double-stop bend that melts into an E minor pentatonic phrase. This gives way to an open E string in prep for another anticipation with a G#/B (3rd/5th) slide. Measure 2 thematically repeats the single-note phrase a 4th lower, based in E Mixolydian, utilizing the open-B string in prep for another E/G# (root/3rd) double stop. Measure 3 changes positions via a chromatic double-stop descent and hammers into an arpeggiated E/G# triad in measure 4 before sliding into a D/F# 6th dyad, which sets up the A chord change by implying E9.

Measure 5 slides into a C#/E (3rd/5th) open-string double stop and pulls off through the A blues scale with a G/B open-string dyad in between. Measure 6 slides into a speedy, A major pentatonic run that climbs the neck through an A7 arpeggio at the fifth position before reaching the ninth-position root note of the E chord in measure 7. Here begins a welcome breather from the technical onslaught with a series of pedal steel bends that cover up an otherwise E major pentatonic, Southern rock cliché.

Measures 9–12 over the B and A chords have transposable identical phrases of the Mixolydian variety, replete with sliding double stops and chromatic, 16th-note pull-offs for a consistent four-measure statement. The terminal slide into the A chord's ♭7th (measure 12) brings interesting contrast to the B chord's ending on the root in measure 10 while perfectly setting up the G# slide into the E chord of measure 13.

An E major pentatonic melody dances toward a punchy G#/B double-stop bend that anticipates and stutter-plucks its way through measure 14. Measure 15 ends the proceedings with another hybrid-picked double-stop descent into a tricky four-note pull-off that quickly turns into a major pentatonic position-shift and speedily runs its way up to a G#/B double-stop bend for the ensemble hit in measure 17.

 TRACK 87

CONCLUSION: WHERE TO GO FROM HERE

The unique sound of country guitar has been an ever-evolving adaptation of sounds that were originally foreign to the instrument. The phrasing vocabulary has taken hints from all styles—be it bluegrass, blues, jazz, rock, and even Latin music. I suppose it's called "country" music because of its utilization of influences from all across the United States—the high lonesome sound of Appalachia, the fast train beats of West Virginia, the pristine arranging techniques of New York and Los Angeles, the Cajun rhythms of Louisiana, and the raw twang of Nashville honky-tonks. To further this tradition of adaptation with your guitar playing, here are some recommendations for further study.

- **Transpose All Licks to Other Keys and Positions**: Moving your ideas to other keys and positions will help ingrain the connections within the fretboard's geography, hone your ears to recognize intervals, and allow you to fluidly add your favorite ideas into your solos wherever you are on the neck.

- **Listen to Other Instruments**: The majority of the techniques presented in this book are inspired by other instruments to create truly unique sounds on the guitar. Pedal steel, fiddle, and mandolin solos are chock-full of inspiring phrasing and licks that are standard repertoire for those instruments, but incorporating those idioms into your guitar playing adds a refreshing twist to your solos.

- **Assimilate Your Influences**: Fluidly mixing disparate influences in a single musical statement eventually leads to innovation of the genre. Brad Paisley's use of Van Halen-inspired legato and Brent Mason's pedal steel lines infused with Latin rhythms are part of their undeniable stylistic signature. Melding together different ideas helps define and solidify your own unique voice on the instrument.

Taking a lesson from the masters and expounding on them to make something truly original is the symbiotic nature of the life-long pursuit of music. Hopefully, *How to Play Country Lead Guitar* has been an insightful and horizon-broadening resource as your path to fully expressing yourself on the instrument continues. Enjoy the journey!

SUGGESTED LISTENING

Some of the most important players in country music have inspired the musical examples in this volume. Keeping these recordings to myself would be a disservice to their genius and your musical growth, so prepare to drown your ears with the greats.

MERLE TRAVIS

Father of the thumbstyle technique that bears his name, he introduced the world to the guitar as a simultaneous rhythm and lead instrument.

Notable Songs: "Cannon Ball Rag" and "Saturday Night Shuffle."

CHET ATKINS

Expounding on the Travis picking technique by incorporating all his fingers, "Mr. Guitar's" open-string innovations and dazzling solo arrangements certified his guitar playing when he wasn't busy inventing the "Nashville Sound."

Notable Songs: "When You Wish Upon a Star," "Mister Sandman," and "Stars and Stripes Forever."

JAMES BURTON

Credited as the creator of chicken pickin', James Burton's tenure with Rick Nelson solidified his country stardom as a prominent session player throughout his career. And, oh yeah: he was also the iconic lead guitarist for the King.

Notable Solos and Albums: "Susie Q," "Suspicious Minds" (Live), and *Rick Is 21*.

ALBERT LEE

With a resume of sessions stretching from the who's who of country to Eric Clapton, Albert's single-note lines and innovative use of delay sent players to the woodshed when his song "Country Boy" hit the airwaves.

Notable Solos and Albums: "Country Boy," *Hiding*, "Luxury Liner," and "Foggy Mountain Breakdown" (with Earl Scruggs and Friends).

VINCE GILL

Gill became the first triple-threat that mixed a tenor voice, a heartfelt songwriting style, and a stunning array of licks that was at home with break-neck, double-time solos as well as evocative ballad duets.

Notable Solos: "Liza Jane," "One More Last Chance," "What the Cowgirls Do," and "Oklahoma Borderline."

BRENT MASON

Lauded as the most-recorded guitarist in history, his hooks and solos defined the hits of Alan Jackson, Brooks & Dunn, and George Strait, effectively inventing the sound of '90s country.

Notable Solos and Albums: *Hot Wired,* "I Don't Even Know Your Name," and "Mercury Blues" by Alan Jackson; "We'll Burn That Bridge" and "My Next Broken Heart" by Brooks & Dunn; and "Lovebug" by George Strait.

BRAD PAISLEY

To match his tongue-in-cheek songwriting style, Brad's oblong licks and G-Bender tricks reinvigorated the pop-rock climate of 21st-century country music with rock-inspired ideas.

Notable Solos and Albums: "Me Neither," "Little Moments," *Play*, and "Mud on the Tires."

OTHER NOTABLE PLAYERS

Johnny Hiland

Ray Flacke

The Hellecasters (John Jorgensen, Will Ray, and Jerry Donahue)

Steve Wariner

Marty Stuart

Pete Anderson

ABOUT THE AUTHOR

Jeff Adams' writing, teaching, and performance experience has afforded him the ability to deftly adapt to a wide range of opportunities within the music business—from transcribing for Keeley Electronics and Gibson Guitars and contributing rock and country-style articles to *Premier Guitar* magazine, to serving as the International Product Specialist and Lead Transcriber for BandFuse: Rock Legends (a guitar-based video game that was applauded by *Guitar World* magazine). With all of this behind him, Jeff considers *How to Play Country Lead Guitar* the culmination of his first 10 years of professional experience and he's proud to offer the secrets behind the style that inspired him to play.

If you'd like to share your experiences with country guitar, e-mail him at *srvincarnate@hotmail.com* and check out Professional Guitar Transcriptions (*www.freewebs.com/powerscribe*).

Guitar Instruction
Country Style!
from Hal Leonard

CHICKEN PICKIN' • *by Eric Halbig* **INCLUDES TAB**

This book provides a "bird's-eye-view" of the techniques and licks common to playing hot, country lead guitar! Covers over 100 hot country guitar licks: open-string licks, double-stop licks, scales, string bending, repetitive sequences, and chromatic licks. CD includes 99 demonstration tracks with each lick performed at two tempos.

00695599 Book/CDPack...$16.95

COUNTRY CLASSICS FOR GUITAR • *arr. Fred Sokolow* **INCLUDES TAB**

30 favorites arranged for solo guitar, including: Always on My Mind • Blue Eyes Crying in the Rain • Crazy • Folsom Prison Blues • If You've Got the Money (I've Got the Time) • Make the World Go Away • Rocky Top • Walking the Floor over You • Your Cheatin' Heart • and more.

00699246...$14.95

FRETBOARD ROADMAPS – COUNTRY GUITAR **INCLUDES TAB**

The Essential Patterns That All the Pros Know and Use • *by Fred Sokolow*

This book/CD pack will teach you how to play lead and rhythm in the country style anywhere on the fretboard in any key. You'll play basic country progressions, boogie licks, steel licks, and other melodies and licks. You'll also learn a variety of lead guitar styles using moveable scale patterns, sliding scale patterns, chord-based licks, double-note licks, and more. The book features easy-to-follow diagrams and instructions for beginning, intermediate, and advanced players.

00695353 Book/CD Pack...$14.99

FOR MORE INFORMATION, SEE YOUR LOCAL MUSIC DEALER,
OR WRITE TO:

HAL•LEONARD®
CORPORATION

7777 W. BLUEMOUND RD. P.O. BOX 13819 MILWAUKEE, WI 53213

Visit Hal Leonard Online at www.halleonard.com
Prices, contents, and availability subject to change without notice.

COUNTRY LICKS FOR GUITAR **INCLUDES TAB**

by Steve Trovato and Jerome Arnold

This unique package examines the lead guitar licks of the masters of country guitar, such as Chet Atkins, Jimmy Bryant, James Burton, Albert Lee, Scotty Moore, and many others! The accompanying CD includes demonstrations of each lick at normal and slow speeds. The instruction covers single-string licks, pedal-steel licks, open-string licks, chord licks, rockabilly licks, funky country licks, tips on fingerings, phrasing, technique, theory, and application.

00695577 Book/CD Pack..............................$17.99

COUNTRY SOLOS FOR GUITAR **INCLUDES TAB**

by Steve Trovato

This unique book/CD pack lets guitarists examine the solo styles of axe masters such as Chet Atkins, James Burton, Ray Flacke, Albert Lee, Scotty Moore, Roy Nichols, Jerry Reed and others. It covers techniques including hot banjo rolls, funky double stops, pedal-steel licks, open-string licks and more, in standard notation and tab with phrase-by-phrase performance notes. The CD includes full demonstrations and rhythm-only tracks.

00695448 Book/CD Pack..............................$17.95

RED-HOT COUNTRY GUITAR

by Michael Hawley

The complete guide to playing lead guitar in the styles of Pete Anderson, Danny Gatton, Albert Lee, Brent Mason, and more. Includes loads of red-hot licks, techniques, solos, theory and more.

00695831 Book/CD Pack...$17.95

25 GREAT COUNTRY GUITAR SOLOS **INCLUDES TAB**

by Dave Rubin

Provides solo transcriptions in notes & tab, lessons on how to play them, guitarist bios, equipment notes, photos, history, and much more. The CD contains full-band demos of every solo in the book. Songs include: Country Boy • Foggy Mountain Special • Folsom Prison Blues • Hellecaster Theme • Hello Mary Lou • I've Got a Tiger by the Tail • The Only Daddy That Will Walk the Line • Please, Please Baby • Sugarfoot Rag • and more.

00699926 Book/CD Pack...$19.99

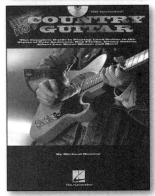
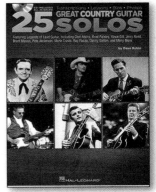